THE FUTURE OF AUTOMOTIVE RETAIL

STEVE GREENFIELD
FOUNDER AND CEO OF AUTOMOTIVE VENTURES

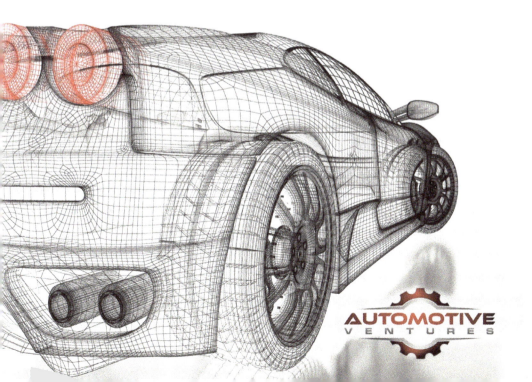

Copyright © 2022 by Steve Greenfield

All rights reserved. No part of this publication may be reproduced, distributed or transmitted in any form or by any means, including photocopying, recording or other electronic or mechanical methods, without the prior written permission of the publisher, except in the case of brief quotations embodied in critical reviews and certain other noncommercial uses permitted by copyright law.

Steve Greenfield/Automotive Ventures LLC
1922 Wildwood PL NE
Atlanta, Georgia 30324
www.automotiveventures.com

The Future of Automotive Retail / Steve Greenfield — 1st ed.
Print ISBN: 979-8-9864718-0-8
eBook ISBN: 979-8-9864718-1-5

CONTENTS

Chapter One - The Future According to Monty 1

Chapter Two - The Convenience Economy 15

Chapter Three - Power Sources 37

Chapter Four - Vehicle Production 67

Chapter Five - Vehicle Ownership 87

Chapter Six - Autonomy 103

Chapter Seven - The Connected Car 131

Chapter Eight - Service and Repairs 157

Chapter Nine - The Future of the Dealership 183

Epilogue - The Calf-Path 211

Acknowledgements 215

Notes 217

CHAPTER ONE

THE FUTURE ACCORDING TO MONTY

"We always overestimate the change that will occur in the next two years and underestimate the change that will occur in the next ten. Don't let yourself be lulled into inaction."
— **Bill Gates, founder of Microsoft**

As Monty surveyed the nearly empty showroom, he couldn't help but reflect on how much circumstances had changed since his mother had bought the dealership thirty years earlier.

A visitor from the past — the now-distant 2020s — might be forgiven for not even recognizing that this was a place that sold cars. Instead of a lot and a showroom full of vehicles, most everything is done digitally nowadays. Shoppers configure and choose their cars from the convenience of their own homes and, for 90% of vehicles, the purchase is delivered to the buyer's driveway. There's barely a need to visit a dealer.

By 2050, the number of customers interested in owning their own vehicles had plummeted. Since the passing of the 2045 Autonomous Vehicle Act, which essentially outlawed human drivers in order to save lives, reduce city congestion and clean up the environment, purchase patterns had shifted wildly, with the majority of cars now being "owned" as part of a subscription plan.

Monty still felt an affinity to ownership — he was a car dealer, after all — and had purchased his current ride — a retrofitted autonomous version of a Volvo SUV with cameras, radar and vehicle-to-vehicle communication — five years earlier, mainly to shuttle him to and from work before sending the vehicle racing back to the home in the Boston suburbs he shared with his wife, Emerson, and their two children, Joel, 4, and Ruthie, 2, to get them to work and school on time.

All vehicles by this time were electric, except for the occasional hydrogen-powered car (which created a cordial if sometimes heated debate between the electro mainstream and the hydrogen nerds as to which was better for the environment). Fueled by stimulus payments to both consumers and manufacturers, the last internal combustion engine (ICE) cars rolled off the assembly lines in 2035, accelerated by General Motors CEO Mary Barra's declaration that GM would end the sale of gasoline-powered cars that year.

A few gas-guzzlers still crawled the streets, but consumers reacted with disdain at the noise and pollution they produced. Other than a small minority of diehard enthusiasts, who eagerly ate up anything with "ICE" in the title, most of those cars had migrated to auto shows, car races or — in a Mad Max kind of twist — the new rage of demolition derbies that had displaced horse racing as the betting person's pastime at the midpoint of the 21st century.

As Monty moved to lock up the showroom after a mostly customer-free but nevertheless long day, much of it spent swiping (or to be more accurate for the year 2050, nodding) right and left on leads using his AR (augmented reality) glasses, he felt a pang of longing.

His mother had raised him on bedtime stories describing the crowds that used to descend on the dealership on weekends. The excited salespeople knew that, with just the right turn of a well-crafted if not entirely transparent phrase, they could squeeze an extra few dollars out of a customer. It was unpleasant for the consumer, of course, but Monty still looked back on those days with a degree of fond nostalgia.

Monty's autonomous Volvo was waiting patiently — without a grumpy driver honking or texting to cajole his would-be passenger to hurry up — and as he hopped in, the vehicle seamlessly scanned his retina before greeting him with its charming if creepily prescient voice.

"Good evening, Monty. Are you headed home now, or would you like to stop at the bakery on the way? There's a sale on Emerson's favorite chocolate ganache cake. And Joel's birthday is this weekend. Have you picked up the candles yet?"

Monty swiped through his recent purchases list on the floor-to-ceiling screen that was his visual home away from home for the forty-five-minute ride from work. Monty hadn't been as fortunate as some who had been able to flex their time, spending most days working from home, a remnant of the 2020 pandemic that had created lasting societal changes still in place some thirty years later.

Fortunately, he had chosen to upgrade his entertainment and e-commerce subscription at the beginning of the month. In a move that was financially lucrative for dealerships, after years of hemming, hawing and obfuscating, most of the surviving OEMs — electric vehicle manufacturers like Tesla, Rivian, NIO and the few American manufacturers that had not been bought out by the Chinese — had finally agreed to share 20% of the revenue from these kinds of over-the-air (OTA) updates with dealers like Monty who still had responsibility for fulfilling, delivering and servicing the cars.

Monty knew that he could turn off the advertising functionality in his car with another upgrade (and an additional monthly fee), but he felt it important to understand what the average car owner experiences.

Monty wasn't thinking about any of that as he loosened his tie for the commute home. He was looking forward to watching an episode or two of his favorite old-school comedy, *Seinfeld,* a remnant from another decade, that helped pass the time.

CHAPTER ONE 3

"No soup for you," he chuckled to himself, anticipating the scene where Jerry and Elaine were rudely ejected from their favorite lunch joint.

"I didn't catch that," his car's system interrupted. "Would you like to stop at the Boston Chowda Co. for that minestrone that Emerson loves?"

"No thanks. I'd like to get home in time to see the kids before Emerson tucks them into bed," Monty said to no one in particular. "But you can go and pick up the candles after I get home."

"Sure, I'll message the store and swing by this evening," the car replied. In the autonomous future, cars doubled as personal assistants, fetching everything from groceries to dry cleaning and birthday cakes.

Emerson, meanwhile, had gotten into a fight that morning with Joel and was still reeling from the enhanced cortisol levels that only a four-year-old can stimulate. Joel was refusing to switch on his cognitive implants, without which he would have had a tough time following what his kindergarten teacher was saying. They were learning basic math, and the exercises were based on intracranial visualization.

Joel eventually acceded to his mother's wishes — but only after Emerson had agreed to allow Lex, the family's walking, talking robotic assistant, to accompany him in the car and escort him to his classroom. (Emerson simultaneously breathed a sigh of relief mixed with a slight sting of sadness — was she already being replaced by a synth?)

At two years old, Ruthie was less combative — as long as she had her holographic Powerpuff Girls doll, she didn't care where she was off to. Lex helped both children get dressed and packed their lunches. Lex did the assembling while Joel and Ruthie egged on their AI companion. ("More insect protein in my sandwich, please!" Joel giggled.)

Emerson was happy for all the time-saving conveniences even if Lex was not quite Rosey the Robot from *The Jetsons* TV show and their autonomous vehicle couldn't fly. The seeds for Lex were sown when Tesla chairman Elon Musk announced the prototype of a "Tesla Bot," designed to eliminate "dangerous, repetitive and boring tasks" like bending over to pick up something or going to the store for groceries, Musk told reporters at Tesla's 2021 AI Day.

Emerson knew, too, that had she been born a decade or two earlier, she'd have had to study and pay for driving lessons. By 2050, hardly anyone had a license. Her husband, Monty, did, but what kind of a car salesman would he be without one?

Still, it was hard to complain: The reduction of pollution, the near elimination of traffic jams, the increased safety while driving in an autonomous vehicle, had contributed to an extended average life expectancy in the United States of an impressive 105 years of age. So much time — how would they fill it?

Surveying her little ones, Emerson wasn't worried.

As Monty's vehicle was getting closer to home, a new message appeared on the wraparound screen. The left front tire was low on air, it read.

Dang. They must have run over something, or maybe it was a pothole. Still, it was strange, Monty thought. Most streets were in great shape, thanks to the data amassed by the millions of connected cars that was automatically shared with municipal planners who could then rush to repair potentially hazardous highways.

"Do I have enough to get home?" Monty asked the vehicle.

"Yes, Monty," the vehicle replied. "I'll take care of this after you've settled in. Which service center would you like to use?"

That was an easy one: Monty's dealership, of course! With sales of vehicles dropping due to the combination of autonomy and subscription models, and a good chunk of sales bypassing dealers entirely in the years since Tesla cracked state regulations allowing manufacturers to sell directly to consumers, Monty had pivoted to focus on service and ancillary services. The range of offerings Monty's dealership offered now was quite different than when his mother ran the place.

Autonomous and electric vehicles didn't need the same level and frequency of service as their predecessors did, but these were still complex machines that required care from time to time.

Most dealers now offered some mix of the following:

- **Charging** — Monty's dealership had a bank of a dozen high-speed charging spots out back. Every night, some five hundred self-driving cars would pull in on their own (a freaky sight, with driverless cars hogging the highways heading to where no one really knew) and connect up for a charge before returning to their owners. That said, now that electric cars could run for close to 2,000 miles between a charge, range anxiety had long since become a nonissue.
- **Cleaning** — Especially for ride-share vehicles, who was going to pick up all the trash and make sure the car was sanitized if not Monty's dealership?
- **Routine maintenance** — With vehicles already visiting dealerships at night on their own, problems could be caught right away rather than at an annual visit. Recalls were becoming rare.
- **Emergency repairs and service** — This had become even more convenient and fast now that so many components could be 3D-printed at the dealership, rather than needing to be ordered and shipped from a central distribution facility.
- **Sensor calibration** — This was necessary so that autonomous cars would always stay in tip-top (and safe) shape.
- **Predelivery inspections** — Even though most car purchases now took place online and in customers' driveways, Monty had positioned his dealership as a smart distribution hub. Despite decades of disruptive forces, the dealership still had relevance!

Almost home, a self-driving bus passed Monty in the furthest left autonomous-only lane on the freeway. Its passengers, seen through the window, looked productive, although it was hard to say — who could know, really, what was going on behind those smart glasses and cognitive implants? Surreptitiously eavesdropping at your neighbor's screen was a quaint remnant of the 2020s.

Ruthie was in the bath with Lex at her side when Monty arrived. Joel had his VR glasses strapped on and was frolicking in a virtual world of brightly colored Virtual Teletubbies. Emerson was in the kitchen 3D-printing vegan burgers for dinner. She was excited to try a new flavor topper: wasabi and cheddar. Monty was less thrilled, but he'd long ago learned not to question Emerson's 21st-century culinary choices.

With the kids and his wife engaged otherwise, Monty gestured toward the living room window, which switched from transparent to opaque to display the evening's headlines. President Maisy Biden was speaking excitedly about the next stage of her grandfather's ambitious infrastructure plan: the terraforming of Mars, which now had a steady stream of space tourists, thanks to the persistence of Griffin Musk, who had taken over from his father following the latter's untimely death in 2030 during a malfunctioning Level 5 autonomous Tesla test in Arizona.

Monty called up his profit and loss spreadsheet on the big screen, a ritual he did most nights before turning from fortune to family. His dealership was doing surprisingly well; the ancillary income had balanced out the lower revenue from sales, and with so few humans working (software and robots could handle 75% of most problems), there was little fat to trim.

Monty was proudest of his dealership's "creativity corner," a take on Apple's still-popular Genius Bars, which had transformed his dealership into a hub of activity during the day. With free, high-quality coffee ("Starbucks on steroids," Monty was fond of saying) and unlimited doughnuts (gluten-free, vegan and reduced-calorie versions available), Monty wasn't always sure if he was selling cars or a WeWork-style "experience."

It hadn't been easy coping with all the changes, but the dealership was profitable, so Monty was satisfied.

With the kids finally in bed, Monty and Emerson were ready for date night. They were both suckers for live entertainment, even as their friends rarely left the comforts of their 4D TVs at home. Lex doubled as babysitter — a more attentive and thoughtful caretaker than Grandma, Monty admitted to no one out loud — so the young couple gestured for the car to come around and take them to a club downtown where Dan Reynolds, the sole remaining member of Imagine Dragons, was working on a comeback tour. (The band peaked with 2012's "Radioactive," but their most loyal fans refused to give up.)

On the way, Monty and Emerson argued amiably over what music the car should play — Emerson loved R&B from the 1960s, while Monty was a fan of mid-'80s Brit-pop. (Neither could stomach the trip-hop stylings of the current era.) Still, their disagreement was nothing like the fights that Monty's mother and father used to have in the car over driving directions.

GPS combined with autonomy was as highly effective as a marriage counselor, it seemed — as was the 3D food printer in the car, which whipped up some healthy snacks for the ride over and kept them hot in its integrated warming box. Emerson discreetly turned off the car's background health monitoring function (another over-the-air upgrade) — did she really want the car telling her that she shouldn't have the extra-spicy mayo with her onion rings or that her BMI was trending a tad high?

The door-to-door service was a delight, as was the lack of any need to circle endlessly around the block in a fruitless attempt to find parking. Monty and Emerson danced with abandon at the club and had one too many mojitos before their self-driving chauffeur deposited them, tired but happy, at home, ready to catch a few hours of shut-eye before starting another tech-driven day.

BACK TO REALITY

Monty and Emerson are fictional characters, of course, but their story highlights the questions, ambivalence and anxiety confronting the automotive retail space as it evolves toward an unknown future.

Among the questions to ponder are these:

- How will the trends we see today, in 2022, evolve into the future of 2050 — or are they preparing us for an alternative future?
- Can we avoid massive disruption? Or should we — *must* we — embrace it?
- How does the future look for dealers, OEMs and consumers in a world where autonomous and electric vehicles rule the streets and dealerships have shrunk to the size of small offices?
- What happens if (or is it more a matter of when?) big tech players like Amazon or Apple get into the automotive retail space, either on their own or through an acquisition? What threats may be coming out of left field?
- What are the best bets for investors in the emerging automotive and mobility space?
- Will car manufacturing change forever as data enables OEMs to make smarter decisions?
- How has the advent of the internet changed the foundational building blocks of automotive retailing?
- And finally, how can all the different stakeholders in the automotive retail space prepare to ensure they not only survive, but also thrive?

In this book, I aim to serve as your guide to an imagined future. We won't be going as far forward as thirty years, but we will dive deep into the world of five and ten years from now.

Author and futurist William Gibson wrote in 2003, "The future is already here. It's just not evenly distributed."

I believe that keenly observing current trends and extrapolating these out five or ten years will allow us effectively to see the future in the automotive space.

This book will guide us there.

We will explore eight broad themes that illustrate the immense challenges facing the industry.

BOOK THEMES

1. The convenience economy
2. Vehicle power sources
3. Vehicle production
4. Vehicle ownership
5. Autonomy
6. Connectivity
7. Servicing of vehicles
8. The future of dealerships

1. **The convenience economy** — How will car sales change in the convenience economy? Will Carvana, Vroom and other direct-to-consumer sales become the norm? What's next for digital retailing and marketplaces? Will Lithia become a force for dealers to reckon with?
2. **Vehicle power sources** — Will it be electric, hydrogen, solar, in-road power or something else entirely? What new battery technology is coming? What do we need to consider about charge-point infrastructure and the impact on the grid?
3. **Vehicle production** — Can technology allow OEMs to manufacture only the cars consumers want and deliver them to the right locations? How will the 2021/2022 chip shortage affect supply, and will this be a long-term problem? How can OEMs and dealers work out their differences?
4. **Vehicle ownership** — Will the future be about individual ownership? Subscriptions? Will you get your next car from a fleet, especially if it's electric?

5. **Autonomy** — When will we see full autonomy on the streets? Will drivers be banned? Will robo-taxis take off? Can Tesla repurpose EVs coming off lease as autonomous vehicles?
6. **Connectivity** — When a feature is unlocked through an over-the-air (OTA) update, who gets the revenue: the dealer, the OEM or both? What kind of privacy permissions will consumers be willing to grant in exchange for in-car personalization? How can municipalities use the data from connected cars to improve city infrastructure?
7. **Servicing of vehicles** — Service and repairs have long been more profitable, with higher margins, than the actual sale of a car. How can dealers enhance what they offer consumers in this area? Will driveway repairs become a thing? What happens to the Jiffy Lubes and Midas repair shops of America?
8. **The future of dealerships** — What new revenue streams can dealers tap into or develop? How will the lines between retail and wholesale blur? What new F&I products will play nicely with online sales? How can dealers deliver on the Amazon "everything by tomorrow" promise?

WHO DID I WRITE THIS BOOK FOR?

If you're an entrepreneur, dealer, OEM, investor or vendor involved with the automotive industry, this book is for you. Pre-COVID-19, dealership profit margins were being compressed due to several factors, a trend that is likely to continue. There are disruptive themes emerging that will impact dealers, automakers and vendors to varying degrees, with uncertain timelines.

How can we better anticipate the timing and magnitude of these challenges and opportunities? How will the automotive retail space look in five, ten and thirty years from now?

About me: I have loved cars since I was a kid and my father used to race competitively. (I do too: My personal land speed record was 180

CHAPTER ONE   **11**

miles per hour on a Yamaha R1 at Road Atlanta.) My father and I spent many weekends together in the family garage, replacing transmissions or the "top end" of an engine.

That eventually led to a career of more than twenty years in the automotive technology space. I started by selling software to car dealers at a Manheim location back in 1999, and ended up overseeing the company's overseas investments, including establishing new joint ventures in Dubai, Istanbul and Beijing.

At Autotrader, I oversaw the acquisitions of vAuto, Kelley Blue Book, HomeNet Automotive and VinSolutions.

I then moved to TrueCar to manage strategy and acquisitions, which is when we acquired DealerScience.

I established Automotive Ventures to help automotive and mobility entrepreneurs raise money, grow and ultimately exit their businesses. We launched an early-stage venture capital fund focused on automotive and mobility startups. I am also a managing director at Progress Partners, a Boston-based investment bank.

My aim is to provide the trusted resources I wished I had as an entrepreneur and investor.

In my spare time, I serve on the Emory College Alumni Board in Atlanta, where I'm based. My Emory connections go deeper: I sit on the board of the Emory Impact Investing Group (EIIG) and the board of the Emory Entrepreneur Network.

Other board positions include T-Drill, Lender Compliance Technologies, RoboTire and Community Consulting Teams (CCT) Atlanta.

I haven't given up my love for fast rides: These days, on weekends, you'll often find me on the racetrack, on one of my three motorcycles.

I don't think it's an exaggeration to say that the automotive industry will see more change in the next ten years than it's experienced in the past hundred. I aim to identify some of the issues in this book so that you're better prepared to navigate these changes.

I believe there is a clear path ahead, but it will take progressive thought leadership and proactive action to anticipate and prepare for that future. Those who anticipate change and adapt accordingly will be best positioned to survive — and ultimately to prosper.

CHAPTER TWO

THE CONVENIENCE ECONOMY

"We see our customers as guests to a party, and we are the hosts. It's our job every day to make every important aspect of the customer experience a little bit better."
— **Jeff Bezos, founder and executive chairman of Amazon**

Drive down the highway in any of twenty-six cities, from Tempe, AZ, to Philadelphia, PA, and you will likely see a stylish tower filled to the brim . . . with cars.

Pop a coin into the control unit at the base of the tower, and the twelve-story unit spins to life — a giant jukebox that whirs and clicks until the car of your choice (one of forty-three in the vending machine) makes its way to the bottom, ready for you to take ownership and drive away.

Carvana is the poster child for the wave of change hitting the automotive retailing world. No longer do you need to go into a physical dealer to haggle on price and be subjected to high-pressure sales tactics just to be upsold features and products you don't want or need.

With Carvana — along with Cazoo, Shift, Vroom and others — you complete the entire car purchase online, then wait for the car to be delivered to your driveway (only a small fraction of Carvana's sold vehicles are picked up at one of their hulking jukebox towers).

Concerned about the lack of the traditional test drive? No problem: You have seven days and 400 miles to pilot your car; if you don't want to keep it, you can return it and get your money back, no questions asked.

This may sound like some far-off future. But the Amazonification of car retailing, with home-delivered instant gratification, is happening right now, and it's causing a surge of anxiety for dealers already contending with the debt incurred by their huge footprints and the millions of dollars invested in their showrooms, often at the request of the automotive manufacturers.

Among dealerships' concerns are the following:

- How can dealers today compete with the kind of disruptive convenience that Carvana, Vroom and others offer consumers?
- If they can't beat 'em, should they jump on the train and offer driveway delivery of their own, either building their own technology solutions or using one of the many available "digital retailing" solutions?
- Is it futile to resist, and is the writing on the wall to sell their stores to a savvy partner such as Lithia, which has been aggressively buying up and consolidating dealerships and has its own online initiative under Driveway.com?
- Is online retailing just a fad — accelerated by COVID-19 — or does it represent a systemic change in the way new and used cars are (and will be) bought and sold?
- Has the Carvana model been overhyped, and will emerging omnichannel offerings of dealerships with physical retail locations prove to be the more durable business model?

Let's consider for a moment the mindset of millennials, who in many ways represent the future of the car-buying public.

Millennials "don't hate cars," writes Roy Furchgott in the *New York Times,* referring to that age group's penchant for using ride-sharing services at the expense of vehicle ownership. Rather, "they hate car dealerships."

They hate the showroom visits that can take five hours.

They hate the paperwork and the high-pressure pitches for add-on products, like wheel and tire insurance.

"I dislike the car dealer rigmarole of 'Let me go talk to my manager' and 'Let's go over to the finance department,'" car consumer Will Clark told Furchgott.

It's not inaccurate to say that millennials use Uber and Lyft more than their baby boomer parents and that many have delayed applying for their driver's licenses, compared with older generations for whom receiving a learner's permit at age sixteen was seen as a rite of passage.

Financially strained from school loans and the vicissitudes of an unforgiving job market (the Great Recession and COVID-19 served up a double gut punch to millennials, in particular), combined with continuing work-from-home policies, and with the average new vehicle costing around $50,000, is it any wonder they continue to delay car buying?

Moreover, new vehicle ownership models are expected to gain in popularity in the coming years, further shaking up traditional buying patterns. Numerous startups are working on car subscriptions, for example — a kind of leasing on steroids — that bundle in the monthly car rental, insurance, roadside assistance, bridge and HOV (carpool) lane tolls, and repairs into one price with the option to swap cars every few months (although in practice, most people keep their cars for, on average, eighteen months).

We will dive into the promise — and challenges — of car subscriptions in a later chapter.

And yet, countering the prevailing wisdom, perhaps as a sign of their growing numbers and coming of age, millennials, it turns out, are in fact buying cars — in 2020, they bought more new cars than any other age group, accounting for 32% of total new car sales, according to the market research firm J.D. Power. Millennials edged out baby boomers for the first time ever.

They're just not doing it like their parents did.

Cars.com reports that millennials are nearly twice as likely to shop for and buy a vehicle entirely online.

"Younger generations want to do more online — Gen Z even more than millennials," Dan Mohnke, Nissan's vice president for e-commerce, told the *New York Times*.

CONVENIENCE VERSUS PRICE

What's driving millennials online? A growing consumer preference that values convenience over money. You can see that with driveway-delivered cars, such as those from Carvana, which are not as cheap as you'd typically find if you went straight to a dealer or bought directly from another owner via an online marketplace.

Nor will the convenience economy be limited to the purchase of a new or preowned vehicle. Maintenance — routine or emergency — will become part of the mix too. After all, why drive your car to a dealer when the dealer could simply dispatch an employee to your home to pick up the car, take it in for service and return it later that day or, even better, send over a mechanic to perform the vehicle service in your driveway?

"People expect going into the dealer to be as fast as buying toothpaste on Amazon," Andrew Walser, CEO of Walser Automotive Group and founder of FUSE Autotech, told me. FUSE develops software for dealerships so that any salesperson can control the consumer experience end to end, and not have to rely on the typical in-store process.

Walser has firsthand experience with dealer process inefficiencies.

In 2011, Walser was running a large dealership of his own. "We had eight people in the F&I [finance and insurance] department and still people were waiting two hours before they could talk to someone on a Saturday morning," Walser recalls.

Walser suggests that Apple's retail stores should be held up as an attractive example of what consumers want from their car-buying experience.

"When I need a cable at the Apple store, everyone there's a cashier. I don't even have to stand in a line," Walser notes. "So why can't everyone be a cashier at a dealership, so that if someone is ready to say yes, you just complete the paperwork without the hassle and the wait time?"

Walser adds that, although dealerships that use his company's software are "five to six times faster" than those doing it the old-fashioned way, "that's still not fast enough for the customer."

Management consulting firm OC&C reports in its Global Automotive Disruption Speedometer 2021 survey that, propelled by the COVID-19 crisis, one in four car buyers said they would be happy to purchase online and have the car delivered without seeing it first. In addition, one in three people who have a car that's financed said they would prefer not to arrange for finance in person (i.e., at a dealership).

DIGITAL RETAIL IS NEARLY HERE

As a result, offering a digital retail experience — whether that's buying exclusively online or through an omnichannel approach where consumers select their car and complete the paperwork online, then come into the dealership to finalize and pick up the vehicle — is becoming an imperative for dealers and marketplaces. COVID-19 only accelerated the trend.

Research shows that, within five years in developed markets, as many as 80% of all car deals will include some digital retail elements.

And here's some good news for dealers: So far, margins from digital retail-initiated sales appear to be equal or better than traditional in-store deals, according to online marketplace consultancy the AIM Group. Moreover, the opportunity to use digital retail to drive efficiency is also significant — digital retail can radically improve both buyer engagement and satisfaction.

The Avondale Group, which runs luxury dealerships in North Texas, found that digital retail software users spend thirteen minutes on a dealer's website versus just five minutes on sites that don't have a digital retail option. Leads submitted via a digital retailing platform convert at 6.2%, compared with 1% for "regular" leads.

Smart software can make it easier for dealers to sell a car to someone far away, especially if the digital retailing system can handle differences in taxation, registration and local laws.

Kennedy Gibson, the marketing director of the Avondale Group, notes that since COVID-19 began, digital retailing leads at her dealerships are up 300%, while sales via digital retailing software increased by 240%.

Even as business began returning to normal as the full brunt of the pandemic began to wane, digital retail use hasn't dropped, Gibson adds. "The Holy Grail is a full online transaction" and millennials and Gen Z will enthusiastically embrace digital retail. "Of course, they're transacting online; the majority of their lives have been online."

Complete end-to-end digital retailing has been stymied in some U.S. states that still require a "wet signature," where physical papers must be signed, even if the car is delivered to the buyer's driveway.

Joe Chura, founder and CEO of Dealer Inspire, now owned by Cars.com, doesn't consider the requirement of a wet signature "a big impedance." The bigger issue, he said, is "dealers still wanting customers to come into the dealership to educate them on finance and warranty offerings. Dealers don't want to give up that part of the gross."

A lot of dealers, Walser says, are "still stuck in a time machine," hoping for a return of their offline glory days.

That's not going to be a winning strategy going forward.

A CarGurus survey of 722 shoppers found that 62% would be open to purchasing entirely online and that 30% of car buyers *preferred* to make their purchase fully online. And while most buyers still value the dealership experience, at least to a certain extent, 71% of CarGurus' customers said they want to conduct more steps online (with price negotiations and financing leading the way).

A survey by Cox Automotive found that 47% of its buyers reported doing more steps via the internet than in the past. And the number of car buyers starting a deal online in the U.S. nearly doubled, from 312,000 to 622,000, in the last year.

According to the Cox survey:

DIGITAL RETAILING MAKES DEALERS MORE EFFICIENT

78%
Reduction of time customers spend at the dealership

50%
Reduction in number of steps to complete a deal

59%
Reduction of time dealer staff spend completing deal

38%
Fewer staff required to complete a car deal

Source: Cox Automotive

And yet, dealers have been slow to adopt digital retailing tools and other elements powering the convenience economy.

For example, Cox found that just 59% of franchise dealers — and only 39% of independents — offer home delivery even though many dealers surveyed reported that their online sales are *more* profitable than in-person transactions.

"Dealers are not thinking about digital retail," industry consultant and president of AutoProfit Ed French told me. "They're just trying to survive. COVID-19 made everyone look at digital retailing, but now that demand is back, there's a 'get 'em in here' mentality. The consumer experience has been abandoned."

Dealers may resist the change, but they risk being left behind.

"Unless you can enhance the shopper's experience on the showroom floor to match the convenience, transparency and time savings you promise with an online tool, it is a thin and hollow gesture that will ultimately fail," says Dan Sayer, vice president of e-commerce for Anderson Auto Group in Nebraska.

Digital retailing isn't likely to account for 100% of vehicle sales anytime soon. A survey conducted by professional services firm Deloitte found the following:

FOUR REASONS A CONSUMER WOULD NOT BUY ONLINE

75%	**64%**
I have to see the vehicle before buying it.	I have to test-drive the vehicle.
38%	**37%**
I prefer to negotiate in person.	I don't feel comfortable buying online.

Source: Deloitte

These numbers, I should note, are for the U.S. In Germany and Japan, the percentage of car buyers who are not sure about digital retailing is even higher.

CarMax, the largest retailer of used vehicles in the U.S., offers an omnichannel experience of its own. The company found that only 11% of consumers would opt for driveway delivery. The vast majority of CarMax buyers still appreciate being able to visit a physical dealership before they finalize their deal.

Paul Walser, a Minnesota dealer, former chairman of the National Automobile Dealers Association and brother of Andrew Walser, admits that "gradually there's going to be more and more done digitally. But I don't see a time — at least in the next few years — where the importance of face-to-face contact is going to be eliminated."

Of those who opt for the digital retailing track, Deloitte reports five main reasons, none of which should come as a surprise by this point:

FIVE REASONS A CONSUMER CHOOSES DIGITAL RETAILING

34% Convenience
21% Speed
19% Ease of Use
16% Necessity
10% Ability to avoid going to a dealer

Source: Deloitte

How can consumers be sure that the vehicle they're selecting online will not have hidden blemishes?

Andrew Gordon, who founded and sold DealerScience to TrueCar, suggested I look at Carvana as a best practice.

"They point out all the damage spots on a car on purpose," Gordon told me. "So, if you ask, 'Is there any additional damage on the car?' they can say honestly, 'Hey, we already showed you everything.' Even more important is the money-back guarantee, so you don't have to worry if the car that arrives is different than advertised."

Average dealerships don't have the technology budget of an AutoNation or a Lithia to run their own state-of-the-art website and are forced to choose their website and digital retailing tool from a landscape of third-party software vendors.

While there are sure to be winners and losers among the digital retailing software vendors, I doubt that one player will dominate. Cox made a big bet on digital retailing in 2016 when it acquired Dealertrack.

CHAPTER TWO 23

The bet was that owning the F&I business would lead to dominance in digital retailing.

The theory didn't play out, and smaller digital retail providers — companies such as AutoFi, CarNow, Darwin, Digital Motors, Gubagoo, Roadster and more — have proliferated.

Dealers like choice, and OEMs, despite coming across as heavy-handed at times, actually don't like to force software onto their dealers.

MERGERS AND NEW INITIATIVES

The emphasis on consumer preference and the convenience economy that companies like Carvana have pushed front and center was at least one reason why physical retailer CarMax acquired Edmunds.com for $404 million in early 2021. By grafting Edmunds' third-party marketplace onto CarMax's real-world footprint, CarMax will be better able to acquire consumer vehicles and to present the cars they want in a way that consumers want to buy them.

CarMax will most certainly leverage Edmunds' strong web traffic (sixteen million visits a month) to reduce the cost of customer acquisition. In 2020, CarMax spent $191 million on marketing. CarMax had already been working with Edmunds to develop an online instant-offer tool for sellers of used automobiles, a feature that has proven popular at other automotive websites.

Is the CarMax-Edmunds pair-up a response to the growing popularity of Carvana? It's a fair assumption.

Carvana has been testing listing other dealers' vehicles; the company recently announced plans to list Hertz rental cars on the Carvana site. So the online retailing game is changing at an accelerated pace, and the other players will need to rush to catch up.

Carvana and CarMax are not the only companies with large market caps and the potential to leverage their public currency to enter new areas via mergers and acquisitions. You can see the overall landscape of automotive retailers in this chart:

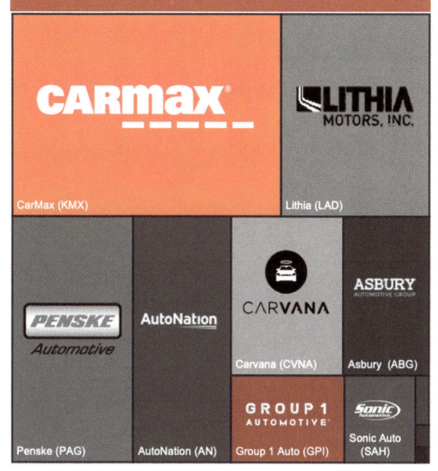

Relative market cap as of May 31, 2022

AutoNation, the country's largest new car seller, is responding to consumer preferences and the convenience economy as well.

Its "AutoNation USA" used-car brand is meant specifically to compete with CarMax and Carvana. With eleven physical locations, an aggressive plan to add new showrooms, plus an online purchase option with driveway delivery, AutoNation USA is touting a one-price "no negotiation" strategy along with two years of free maintenance, including oil change, tire rotation and basic inspection.

Also included in the AutoNation offer are a lifetime's supply of batteries and auto parts at bulk-buy prices.

AutoNation has more than three hundred franchise dealer locations as well as fifteen AutoNation Collision Centers.

All this is ultimately good news for consumers. For dealers, however, the growing traction of Carvana and other driveway delivery services is proving to be an existential threat.

That's created an opening for folks such as Lithia.

The Oregon-based company, which is the second-largest dealer group in the U.S., with some 267 locations in twenty-four states, has been actively buying dealerships over the past several years. In 2020, Lithia began a nationwide rollout of Driveway.com to take on Carvana, Vroom and now CarMax/Edmunds by delivering new and used cars to consumers' homes. All fifty-five thousand vehicles from Lithia's combined dealerships can be purchased online, and delivery covers the entire country. Driveway.com also schedules driveway pickups for maintenance.

Lithia has announced a five-year plan to reach $50 billion in revenue, with the aim of capturing 5% of the $2 trillion U.S. automotive market. (Carvana also has stated its intentions of bumping up its share of the market from 2% today to 5%.) If this goal is realized, Lithia may begin to be rewarded as a high-growth tech company, commanding a market capitalization at a much higher valuation than its peers, and may become much larger, not only than any other dealership group, but also than any supplier and many automakers.

Will they make it? I think they have a good chance.

From my perspective, Lithia is preparing to evolve into the new car version of Carvana. Lithia CEO Bryan DeBoer has stated that their vision is to grow to five hundred physical stores, with a footprint that is within a hundred-mile delivery range of the major population centers in the U.S. market. In addition, I wouldn't be surprised if Lithia transitions their brand to lead with their online-centric shopping experience, Driveway.com.

Once Lithia has a national footprint comprising every OEM brand, it will be able to provide driveway delivery of both new and used vehicles nationwide.

Another acquisition that made the news in 2021, one that was intended to address the convenience economy, was CDK Global's purchase of Roadster for $360 million. Roadster provides dealers with a cross-platform synchronized omnichannel tool to sell new and used vehicles online from the dealer's showroom or at home.

CDK Global is a retail automotive technology company and the largest provider of dealer management systems, with products that include Connected Store, a digital quote, loan and payment tool; and Elead CRM, a lead-generated software platform. Roadster will connect CDK to dealer back-end systems to beef up the end-to-end sales process.

With Carvana blazing a trail around their consumer experience, we are seeing additional marketplaces, both domestically and internationally, attempting to emulate the Carvana experience. While Lithia, CarMax and AutoNation are shaping up to be the "other" elephants in the room, there will undoubtedly be more innovation and acquisition activity ahead.

THE LITHIA ADVANTAGE

Walt DeBoer founded Lithia in 1946 as a Chrysler-Plymouth-Dodge dealership in Ashland, Oregon. Walt's son, Sid, along with Dick Heimann, grew the business to include five stores and nineteen franchises in southern Oregon. (Sid's son Bryan now runs the company.)

In 1996, this collection of dealerships was transformed into the publicly traded Lithia Motors. The company now has dealerships that reach 92% of U.S. consumers. Their goal is to have a dealer within 100 miles of every U.S. car buyer.

Lithia is growing so fast that, unless it is derailed by unforeseen circumstances, it should be double the size of any U.S. dealership group by 2025. The company hopes to realize $13 billion in revenue by that point from annual core operations, another $3 billion to $5 billion from acquisitions, and $9 billion from expanding Driveway.com's e-commerce platform nationally.

In 2020, Lithia acquired Suburban Collection in Michigan — one of the largest deals of its kind in automotive retail history — adding thirty-four new-car dealerships, fifty-six franchises and $2.4 billion in revenue. Lithia also recently moved into Canada with an acquisition of the Pfaff Auto dealership group.

Lithia has incentivized its dealers to make acquisitions in their own backyards.

"Those partners get about twice the amount of stock, and they have full autonomy," Bryan DeBoer explained. "They can use capital to grow and get a second store or third store or fourth store. The rest of the stores are all aspiring to become that."

Autonomy works as long as the Lithia dealerships remain profitable.

"We just want to make sure that you can grow your market share, you grow the loyalty of your customers, and, ultimately, that yields profitability," DeBoer said. "We're not as caught up in how you do it."

As Lithia moves forward, I wouldn't be surprised if the company eventually changes its name to the catchier door-to-door delivery service Driveway.com, which would position the company in the minds of the investment community as a tech company and not just a dealership.

As dealerships contend with continuing margin erosion (a theme I will cover further in subsequent chapters), can the average dealer keep up with Lithia, with its massive budget and growing national footprint? The single mom-and-pop store will be under even more pressure to sell to the larger consolidators.

RELEVANCE OF THE DEALER MODEL

So, are dealers even necessary anymore? Why not buy direct from the manufacturer, as would be the case with many other types of consumer products?

The automobile is "not like the usual product that customers buy 'off the shelf,'" wrote long-time CEO and chairman of GM Alfred P. Sloan Jr. in his autobiography, *My Years with General Motors*. "It is a highly complex mechanical product. It represents a large investment for the average purchaser. He expects to operate it, perhaps daily, yet the chances are he possesses little or no mechanical knowledge. He [therefore] depends upon his dealer to service and maintain the product for him."

That may no longer be true, however, as we enter an age of frictionless shopping online, where automotive retailers are taking a cue on how easy it should be from the Amazon playbook.

Jim Leman, writing for DrivingSales, notes, "A tough grind's ahead for America's dealer body as it restructures to deliver the customer experience consumers demand today. This means radical process, staffing, culture and technology change. It means reinventing the dealership's purpose and function."

He then adds ominously, "It will be too much for many managers and some dealers."

Maryann Keller, a forty-year automotive industry veteran, Wall Street securities analyst and founder of an automotive consulting firm bearing her name, remained a steadfast franchise dealer enthusiast.

"National franchise networks foster competition and therefore ensure fair market pricing in new and used cars and with service," she wrote in the white paper *Consumer Benefits of the Dealer Franchise System*.

The alternative — where OEMs sell directly to the public, much as Tesla is trying to do today — would be disastrous, Keller opines.

"The separation of the retail sale and service functions apart from the design and production of vehicles enables free and open

CHAPTER TWO 29

competition among different brands as well as among dealers of the same brand. This translates into a marketplace where national, regional and local factors are permitted to influence transaction prices."

Keller reminded readers of the failed 1997 "Ford Collection" experiment (originally known as the "Ford Retail Network") where the manufacturer sold cars at fixed prices in five cities: Oklahoma City, Tulsa, Rochester (NY), Salt Lake City and San Diego. Ford consolidated individually owned stores under common ownership, and management and participating dealers received 80% of the equity. Ford was a 20% partner.

But rather than making it easier for consumers, the experiment "resulted in less competition with reduced access to sales and service as some stores were closed in each consolidated market," Keller noted. Ford eliminated fixed prices within two years, "thus demonstrating that the marketplace, not the manufacturer, will set prices."

The experiment was abandoned in 2001.

Keller, always the dealer cheerleader, pointed out that, "Contrary to the uninformed criticism of dealers in the media, there is substantial evidence that car buyers today are very pleased with their dealership experiences buying a car or having their vehicle serviced. To define the role of a dealer as a passive middleman whose only function is to deliver a car at a negotiated price is to not comprehend the various services provided by the dealer to enable the purchase and to maintain the car over its long life."

And yet, even if Keller's assessment was correct, how long can this last in the face of unprecedented disruption?

ANTICIPATE DISRUPTION

In many ways, it's a great time to be an auto dealer, with demand for new and used vehicles outstripping supply and consumers ponying up full price or more for popular models.

But it's also a very unsettling time to be an auto dealer. Disruption is driving that uncertainty.

We are by now accustomed to seeing disruption in different tech fields:

- The iPhone disrupted existing phone players, such as BlackBerry, Nokia and Motorola.
- Netflix disrupted Blockbuster (all the way into bankruptcy).
- Uber and Lyft disrupted the value of a New York City taxi medallion — and upended the taxi business wherever they launched.
- Digital cameras disrupted Kodak's century-long dominance with film and chemicals. (The disruption was doubly destructive since Kodak actually invented the first digital camera in 1975 but refused to invest in it out of a fear it would cannibalize the company's existing business. It eventually did, but not in a way Kodak could control.)
- Classified advertising websites disrupted newspapers nearly out of business. The 2008 downturn only compounded the issue. That's how the New York Daily News came to be acquired in 2017 for all of $1.00 (the buyer assumed all of the paper's operational and pension liabilities).
- The internet and on-screen program listings made publications like *TV Guide* increasingly irrelevant. It, too, was sold for $1.00.

Automotive retailing cannot skirt the challenges of digital disruption, especially in an industry that Andy Bruce, CEO of U.K. car dealer Lookers, quipped in 2015 was second only to visiting the dentist in terms of unpleasantness and lack of control.

Carvana, Vroom and Shift are attempting to evolve the way used cars are sold, to be sure, but for new vehicle sales, we can't discount Tesla, which is working assiduously to tear down state laws prohibiting manufacturers from selling direct to consumers.

Any breakthroughs Tesla achieves will undoubtedly have ripple effects throughout the industry. General Motors is already dipping its toes into the direct sales model with the electric Hummer, which has been sold exclusively online, with the dealer reduced to a delivery point.

Traditional auction companies such as Manheim and ADESA, providing a key behind-the-scenes component of the overall automotive retail ecosystem, are finding themselves aggressively disrupted by new all-digital auction platforms such as ACV Auctions.

TrueCar tried to disrupt the automotive advertising segment with its famous slogan "Never overpay," which was much loathed by dealers, who felt TrueCar was boxing them in to deep discounts with no wiggle room for negotiation.

TrueCar replaced that line — and the business model that went with it — in 2016. The new slogan — "See what others paid" — was watered down, to be sure, but it was a less controversial value proposition and helped TrueCar gain respect back from angry dealers.

The biggest disruptors to the industry may be yet to come, when autonomous and electric battery-powered vehicles gain widespread adoption — autonomy, because it fundamentally shakes up the existing ownership paradigm; electric vehicles, because they have fewer moving parts than gasoline-powered cars and thus need less servicing, a major profit center for dealerships.

"The rule of thumb is that an electric vehicle is going to require about one-third the service needs of an internal combustion engine vehicle," Hyundai Motor America CEO José Muñoz said in May 2021.

California has banned the sale of gasoline-powered cars after 2035. China has set the same date for new rules that allow only electrics or hybrids to be sold. Britain is timing its internal combustion engine ban for 2030.

We'll examine these major trends in greater detail later in the book, in the chapters on electrification and autonomy.

Combine autonomous and electric, and you have a cost reduction and ownership shift threat that fundamentally flips traditional models. Herbert Diess, chairman of Volkswagen, predicts that this "global transformation of the industry will take roughly ten years."

That might be an aggressive timeline, but as energy consultant Daniel Yergin notes, "America's love affair with the car will turn into more of a hookup, with the convenience of a utility."

Is it any wonder that Toyota is rebranding itself as a "mobility company" and Volkswagen has picked the moniker of "software-driven mobility provider"?

Dealerships are not the "types of organizations that are designed to deal with this kind of disruption," notes Mike Granoff, head of transportation-focused venture capital firm Maniv Mobility in Tel Aviv. "It's really the exception where disruption comes and an incumbent player rides the wave well enough to capitalize on it. Not that those opportunities don't exist, but they're more likely to be figured out by innovative third parties before dealers can take advantage of them."

A BRIEF HISTORY OF AUTOMOTIVE RETAIL

The coming automotive retail landscape, driven by powerful forces such as consumer preferences, home delivery and a craving for convenience, is a far cry from how cars have been sold historically.

The first franchise new-car dealership opened in Reading, PA, in 1896. It sold automobiles from the now defunct manufacturer Winton. An independent dealership in Detroit soon offered electric cars — all the rage at the turn of the last century — from manufacturer Waverly.

American inventor George Selden is credited for receiving a patent for "an automobile powered by a gasoline engine" and, for a while, every automobile company was supposed to pay a licensing fee to Selden.

Henry Ford balked, claiming that the engine used in his Model T was a different design from Selden's patent. The court agreed, and in 1911, Selden's licensing requirement was voided. With the Model T rapidly rolling off Ford's assembly lines, the industry truly took off — including the franchise dealer model.

By the 1920s, as cars became a true consumer good (not just for the elite), three separate retail systems emerged: OEM-owned stores, independent distributors under contract with an OEM, and independent franchise dealers.

At its height, the U.S. automotive industry sported some five thousand brands powered by gas, steam and electric batteries. By World War I, just fifty manufacturers had survived, and by 1942, at the dawn of World War II, it was down to a sparse few, including General Motors, Chrysler, Ford and Studebaker.

Imports — at first from Europe and later from Asia — shook things up. The Volkswagen Beetle sold five hundred thousand units in 1965; it proved to be the longest-running and most-manufactured car of a single platform ever made.

Japanese cars took America by storm when the OPEC oil embargo drove the price of gasoline up in the early 1970s; the Japanese made smaller, less gas-guzzling vehicles that have remained popular to this day. Honda and Toyota began selling in the U.S. in the 1950s and 1960s but really hit their stride by 1972 when Toyota sold its one millionth vehicle.

By the end of 1975, Toyota had surpassed Volkswagen to become the No. 1 import brand in the U.S.

By 1970, U.S. new-car dealerships had ballooned to more than thirty thousand. The number dropped by the year 2000 to twenty-two thousand and today hovers at just over seventeen thousand.

The internet, of course, upended everything in an industry that hasn't changed much in over one hundred years. Price transparency, online transactions, lead generation, the shift of classified ads from print to online, price quotes by email — all together, they led to the emergence of an informed shopper no longer at a disadvantage vis-à-vis savvy dealers who'd previously held all the cards.

Franchise dealers today spend over 60% of their new-car advertising budgets online and source some 30% of their business opportunities by purchasing online leads or from online shoppers submitting lead requests through the dealer's (or an online marketplace's) website. Consumers spend sixteen to seventeen hours on average researching their vehicle of choice before arriving at the dealership in person.

THE TAKEAWAY

So what should entrepreneurs, dealers, OEMs, investors and vendors take away from the accelerating emphasis on consumer preference and the convenience economy?

"The 'just go get 'em' sales practices of the '80s and '90s don't work anymore," notes automotive industry consultant and former Buick dealer Ed French. "Instead, today's processes have to mirror and match consumers' desires, meaning knowing how to connect with shoppers where they are in their individual shopping research. Today's meet and greet is often conducted via chat or email, so sales associates may need to start their initial conversation with customers prior to the traditional [face-to-face] engagement point."

The behaviors emerging today — a preference for convenience versus price, moving the bulk of the car-shopping process online and subsequently downsizing the need for over-the-top dealership footprints — will be with us for decades to come, even as changes in technology accelerate.

Continuing margin compression at dealerships will erode historical profit centers, forever altering the economics of owning a showroom. And when autonomous vehicles finally make it to the mainstream, increases in vehicle capacity utilization will greatly reduce new car sales.

Dealers who lack the resources, the ambition or the tolerance for change may elect to cash out (now, while there is still strong demand to acquire dealerships) or will increasingly risk becoming irrelevant, and ultimately — slowly but surely — being forced out of the business.

The upside for wary dealers: There doesn't seem to be any end in sight to the ample number of consolidators seeking to acquire new assets by gobbling up willing sellers.

"If you have access to capital and are driven, if you can be innovative and are willing to operate in a volatile environment, then you can continue to grow," says Cliff Banks, automotive industry consultant and publisher of the *Banks Report*. "If you're older and don't have access to capital, though, now may be the time to get out. You'll never see valuations higher than they are right now."

The bottom line, as in any industry where disruption is coming (or has already arrived): Those who anticipate change and adapt accordingly will be best positioned to survive and ultimately prosper.

Not all the pieces of the convenience economy have come together yet, but when they do, the effects "will be profound," writes Yergin, "just like the first car revolution more than a century ago."

Amazon founder Jeff Bezos put it perhaps best.

"It's impossible to imagine a future ten years from now where a customer comes up and says, 'Jeff, I love Amazon; I just wish the prices were a little higher' [or] 'I love Amazon; I just wish you'd deliver a little more slowly,'" he said in 2017. "And so, the effort we put into those things, spinning those things up, we know the energy we put into it today will still be paying off dividends for our customers ten years from now."

CHAPTER THREE

POWER SOURCES

"If electric vehicle adoption continues to accelerate, EVs are likely to account for more than half of all U.S. passenger car sales by 2030."
— *McKinsey & Company*

Of all the changes coming to the automotive industry, electrification is top of mind for dealerships today. The switch from gasoline-powered to 100% electric battery-powered cars will have a long-lasting and profound impact on the way dealers do business, the way manufacturers design and sell cars and how consumers relate to a rapidly evolving American dream in which owning an internal combustion engine (ICE) vehicle has long been the ultimate status symbol.

Of course, electric batteries are not the only option for weaning consumers away from the emissions of ICE vehicles. Hydrogen, solar and other solutions are all under development. (The Environmental Defense Fund estimates that transportation is responsible for nearly 27% of greenhouse gas emissions.)

But electric vehicle adoption is so far ahead, it's hard to imagine any of the other power sources catching up. Volkswagen, for example, predicts that EV sales will reach parity with ICE vehicles as soon as 2030.

While consulting firms don't agree on the exact timeline for EVs, three notable companies — Ernst & Young, BloombergNEF and the Boston Consulting Group (BGC) — all believe that EVs will make up the vast majority of global vehicle sales somewhere between 2036 and 2040.

E&Y, for example, says that global sales of electric vehicles will reach a tipping point in 2033 with non-EV sales plummeting to less than 1% of the global car market by 2045.

BCG expects just 4% of cars to be gasoline-powered by 2036 (albeit in Europe, not the U.S.). More than half of all light vehicles sold in 2026 will be electric.

The Biden administration, in August 2021, set a voluntary target for 50% of all cars and light trucks sold in the U.S. by 2030 to be electric, hydrogen fuel cell or hybrid vehicles. General Motors, Ford and Chrysler immediately backed the pledge.

The Biden plan also set aside $7.5 billion to construct a nationwide EV charging network, and another $7.5 billion for low- and zero-emissions buses and ferries to replace school buses that run on diesel fuel.

McKinsey notes that, during 2020, China and Europe achieved fourth-quarter EV sales increases of 60% and 80% respectively. Meanwhile, the U.S. saw EV sales jump 200% between the second quarter of 2020 and the same period in 2021. McKinsey forecasts that EV sales will account for some 53% of all passenger car sales by 2030.

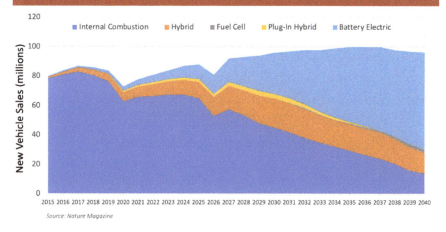

Millennials are driving this EV movement, with 30% of the group born between 1981 and 1997 saying they want to drive electric, according to E&Y.

That said, it's important to point out that, in 2020, electric vehicles represented just 2.3% of total car registrations in the U.S., according to the Automotive News Research & Data Center.

And, as Jay Vijayan, CEO of automotive industry software vendor Tekion (and former chief information officer of Tesla) points out, internal combustion engines will likely coexist with electric vehicles for the foreseeable future, at least in small numbers.

"I don't think there will be a ban [of ICE vehicles] happening in the next ten to twenty years," Vijayan told me.

The numbers may be small today, but that means there's nowhere to go but up.

"The year-over-year increases will look unbelievable because we're starting with such a low number. It will always look like we're climbing," Reilly Brennan, general partner of Trucks Venture Capital, told me.

"Electrification will be virtually ubiquitous in thirty years," adds investor Mike Granoff, head of the Maniv Mobility fund in Tel Aviv. "Think beyond cars. There are also scooters, mopeds, e-bikes. The future of electric vehicles may not look anything like today's cars."

Why are consumers buying (or interested in buying) an EV? Management consulting firm OC&C reports that 57% of the drivers it surveyed would consider purchasing a battery-powered vehicle, up from 43% who considered it for their last car purchase. The budding affection is driven principally by improved perception of range and infrastructure. A smaller percentage (29%) cited worry about the environment as a reason they'd consider an EV.

Would-be buyers still have concerns in four key areas:

CONSUMER EV ANXIETY FROM FOUR SOURCES

RANGE	PRICE
CHARGING AVAILABILITY	SPEED OF CHARGING

OC&C further breaks that down as follows:

WOULD-BE EV BUYERS STILL HAVE CONCERNS

CONCERN	PERCENTAGE
Vehicle Range	60%
Cost to Purchase	46%
Access to Charging Points	46%
Maintenance Costs	28%
Reliability	26%
Cost of Electricity	24%
Resale Value	11%

Source: OC&C Strategy

As far as price sensitivity goes, OC&C found that only 16% of respondents are willing to pay $2,500 more for their electric vehicle; 70% wouldn't pay more than a $500 premium over an ICE vehicle.

CHAPTER THREE   41

A YouGov poll found that, although half of Americans support banning the sales of gasoline-powered cars, only 21% say they would consider buying a fully electric vehicle. Charging time and the hassle of charging were the top-cited reservations.

Eventually, though, concludes Dustin Krause, head of e-mobility for Volkswagen of America (and also a former Tesla executive), "The benefits of EVs are going to become so apparent — it's like broadband compared to dial-up."

"The electric car is here to stay," predicts TV's Jay Leno, the host of CNBC's *Jay Leno's Garage* and a well-known car aficionado. "A child born today will probably drive in a gasoline-powered car about as often as you would drive in a car with a stick shift now."

Let's look at some of the major developments regarding electric vehicles that have caught my attention recently — and that should at once excite and alarm dealers, manufacturers and vendors.

GENERAL MOTORS

In January 2021, General Motors CEO Mary Barra stunned the industry by announcing that GM plans to offer electric vehicles exclusively by 2035, ending production of gasoline- and diesel-powered cars, trucks and SUVs. GM aims to be 100% carbon neutral globally by 2040. As early as 2030, GM is committing to using only renewable energy to power its U.S. facilities. The company is investing $27 billion today in order to release thirty new EV models by 2025.

GM's push into EVs has a long history of ups and downs. The company was once an electric car pioneer, with its introduction of the EV1 in 1996.

The EV1 was a sleek, state-of-the-art car with many of the same features found in today's electric vehicles. GM reportedly spent close to $1 billion to design, produce and market the car, which was adored by its high-profile Hollywood owners, including Mel Gibson and Tom Hanks.

But just a few years after its launch, citing "lack of demand" and high production costs, GM moved aggressively to kill the project. During the car's three-year run, GM sold just 1,117 EV1s and by 2002, had bought back or taken possession of every vehicle it had produced.

And then GM crushed and demolished them all, except for forty cars that were saved for museums — with their electric powertrains demonstratively deactivated.

Given that history, it was somewhat surprising that GM's then vice president of global product development, Bob Lutz, who had spearheaded such gas-guzzlers as the Dodge Viper muscle car, the Chevy Malibu and the Buick LaCrosse, and who had famously once called climate change "a crock of shit," became an electric vehicle champion inside the company.

It was the launch of the Tesla that did it for Lutz.

"That tore it for me," he explained in 2007. "If some Silicon Valley startup can solve this equation, no one is going to tell me anymore that [a car run on lithium-ion batteries] is unfeasible."

Lutz backed the Chevy Volt, a hybrid with a unique approach: Its electric motor could power the car for about 25 miles before it switched over to gas. That was a very different model than most other hybrids, such as the Toyota Prius, which shift back and forth between gas and electric.

The Volt, despite its technological wizardry, never sold particularly well, and so along came the Bolt, Chevy's 100% electric car; it's been struggling as well, in part due to concerns that its battery could spontaneously catch fire, a concern that has led to massive Bolt recalls.

In 2022, an all-electric Hummer and an electric Cadillac SUV called the Lyriq joined the growing list.

Will GM do better with this latest attempt at offering EVs?

TESLA

The success of Tesla can be summed up in one statistic: In 2020, General Motors sold 7.7 million cars and had a market capitalization of

$61 billion. Tesla, meanwhile, makes only 365,000 cars a year and yet has a market cap of over $1 trillion.

GM's Barra has tried to spin the gap.

"I think it points to the opportunity that's in front of us," she told *Freakonomics Radio* host Stephen Dubner in early 2021.

Still, Tesla remains the company to beat with its attractive cars, cult following and flamboyant CEO Elon Musk.

"Tax credits didn't make Tesla," says Granoff, deflecting criticism that Tesla has been propped up less by sales and more by government incentives. "It was a sexier, premium experience that taught consumers that electric didn't have to mean sacrifice, which is what most people thought before 2010. Now it's reached critical mass, where your friends see you with your car. Tesla really succeeded in that."

Tesla now has four main models — the X and Y crossovers, the original S, and the more recent "budget-priced" Model 3. Tesla has another seven vehicles in the pipeline, including two electric battery-powered trucks, an EV van, a revamped four-seat Roadster, and a two-person electric ATV currently dubbed the "Cyberquad."

Lutz summed up Tesla's genius.

"What Tesla got right," he told energy industry consultant Daniel Yergin, "was what everybody else thought was wrong. Everybody else thought electric vehicles should be small, cheap and ugly, and for people who did not want to pay a lot for gasoline. Musk saw that the objective was to get a beautiful stylish car that would go 300 miles on a battery and that cost $100,000."

Tesla has also been changing the rules of the game.

Removing barriers so that Tesla, the manufacturer, can sell directly to the public, rather than via a network of franchise dealers, has been a key struggle, with the company working state by state to change legacy regulations.

Controlling the residual value of Teslas returning from lease has also been part of the strategy.

In a bit of fungible math, Tesla guarantees that when a car on lease comes home, the seller will receive 80% of the original price; that's the "residual value" and it's a key metric for OEMs seeding cars to corporate leases and rental-car agencies. An 80% buyback guarantee also means that the monthly lease payments on a new Tesla can be particularly low, at around $500 a month, the apparent "magic number" that resonates with consumers.

"Tesla understood that the only way to sell cars is to price them low," explains Scott Painter, who founded Fair.com, a car subscription service, and now serves as CEO of Autonomy (formerly NextCar), a similar subscription play. Painter told the *AIM Group Marketplaces Report* that Musk "created that outcome by overinflating the residuals on leasing."

Of course, anyone who's ever bought a new car has heard the adage that a vehicle loses over 20% of its value the second it's driven off the dealer's lot. So how does Tesla justify 80% residual value after three years?

According to Painter, Tesla isn't planning on reselling those cars, but on transforming them into an "autonomous robot fleet" when they come off lease — that is, as a Tesla-branded competitor to Uber.

If true, will it work? It's a big swing, but by this point, industry insiders have learned not to underestimate Elon Musk.

THE FORD F-150 LIGHTNING

Among the most anticipated EVs is the electrified version of the Ford F-150, the company's bestselling pickup truck. The price in the U.S. is just $32,000 for Americans who qualify for the federal EV tax credit. That's a mere $4,000 more than the gasoline-powered version of the F-150 and compares favorably with the average price of $40,000 for a new car in the U.S. The F-150 Lightning gets about the same range as the Tesla Model 3 but costs $7,000 less. (You do have to prefer a pickup truck to a Tesla.)

Ford sells about nine hundred thousand nonelectric F-150s a year. An electric F-150 opens a new and potentially enormous market for

EVs. Moreover, it signals that climate-friendly tech has reached the construction sites of middle America.

The F-150 Lightning has a "Mega Power Frunk," a front trunk, in addition to a back one since the electric engine is smaller and the battery is distributed along the bottom of the vehicle rather than in just one place, like a gas tank. In that "frunk" are multiple plugs for appliances. That could come in handy during a blackout, since Ford says the F-150 Lightning can supply a house's normal power usage for three days. If the house conserves power, it can last for more than a week.

The F-150 Lightning will be available both for consumers and corporate fleet managers (think landscaping companies, HVAC repair people and electricians). These types of users don't typically travel long distances, making this a perfect vehicle for them. The fact that the vehicles are usually stored in the same place every night makes for easier charging. And the lower upkeep costs should make them cost-effective in a fleet.

Reservations for the F-150 Lightning have far outpaced Ford's expectations, to the point where the company decided to cap reservations at two hundred thousand — more than three times Ford's planned annual production — and begin taking actual orders instead.

"The demand for our first round of high-volume EVs clearly has exceeded our most optimistic projections," noted Ford CEO Jim Farley in July 2021.

"This is not a niche play," stressed Jasen Turnbull, marketing manager for the Ford F-150 Lightning, in an interview with TheCarConnection.com.

Ford's electric plans are part of a project called Team Edison, which is also overseeing development of the Mustang Mach-E electric crossover (intended as the first mass-market competitor to Tesla, with thirteen thousand units sold in the first half of 2021, compared with thirty-two thousand gasoline-powered Mustangs) and the 2022 Ford E-Transit electric van.

"We do not assume everyone wants an electric car," Darren Palmer, vice president of Ford's Electric Vehicles Programs, explained. "We want to make electric cars that are so compelling that people have to pay attention and take notice."

NIO AND THE RETURN OF BATTERY SWAP

In 2007, Israeli electric car company Better Place launched an ambitious approach to addressing range anxiety. Instead of plugging in to charge, Better Place built a charging network in Israel and Denmark where drivers would pull into a battery-swapping station. In five minutes, robots would remove the spent battery and replace it with a fresh, fully charged one. The old battery would then be fast charged, ready for the next driver.

Better Place went bankrupt in 2013. Car owners didn't embrace the swap versus charge proposition, and the $850 million Better Place raised wasn't enough to get past such reservations. But that hasn't stopped other companies from trying to improve on the swap experience.

Tesla was the first.

Just a month after Better Place went belly-up, Musk demonstrated a ninety-second battery swap on stage to wild applause. Tesla also built a switching station between Los Angeles and San Francisco.

But drivers gave the idea a decidedly lukewarm response.

"We've invited all the Model S owners in the area to try it out, and of the first round of two hundred invitations, only four or five people were interested," Musk told shareholders and investors in 2015. "Clearly, it's not very popular."

Chinese electric car startup NIO may have figured out the formula.

The company, which has sold about 120,000 vehicles to date, has also built three hundred swapping stations across China, with plans to bump that up to seven hundred by the end of 2021 and four thousand by 2025. NIO said it completed half a million battery swaps in 2020 and is now expanding to its first market outside Asia: Norway (not surprising — see below).

CHAPTER THREE   47

NIO's swapping stations, which are semiportable units akin to a small shipping container and thus don't require digging deep into the ground as with Better Place's infrastructure, come equipped with fourteen battery slots — thirteen for battery packs and an empty slot for discharged batteries. The stations can complete 312 swaps a day, with each exchange taking between five and six minutes. The cars drive themselves into the swap stations using NIO's autonomous navigation technology. Everything is controlled on the user's smartphone.

A NIO portable battery swap station

One of the benefits of NIO's "battery-as-a-service" approach is that drivers can easily upgrade to a battery with greater range. NIO's cars come with either a 70-kWh (kilowatt-hour) or an 85-kWh battery but can receive a 100-kWh battery for a one-time fee of $8,744 or a monthly subscription fee of $133. The 100-kWh battery has a range of nearly 400 miles.

NIO points out that a customer could upgrade to the bigger battery as needed and then return to the original, lower-capacity battery later. And, taking a page from Better Place, there's an option to buy a NIO *with no battery at all* and add the battery for $224 a month. In that case, the cost of the vehicle plunges by nearly $20,000.

NIO also announced plans to run Level 4 autonomous vehicle tests in Tel Aviv using Intel's Mobileye software, with an aim to begin transporting taxi passengers for payment in 2023. We'll discuss that more in the chapter on self-driving cars.

Ample is another startup that hopes to crack the battery-swap conundrum. The company proposes outfitting vehicles with Ample's modular battery packs, which can be swapped out at dedicated stations.

In early 2021, Ample landed a partnership with Uber to use the company's battery-swapping stations at a few locations in the Bay Area. Both companies have agreed to extend their partnership to Europe, where Uber aims to electrify half the rides that are booked across seven European capitals — London, Amsterdam, Brussels, Berlin, Paris, Madrid and Lisbon — by 2025.

THE NORWAY EXPERIMENT

It's no surprise that NIO's first non-Chinese market would be Norway. The Scandinavian country's pro-EV policies — which eliminate the taxes imposed on vehicles powered by fossil fuels, slap a 20% carbon tax on internal combustion engine cars, and include free or reduced-price access to HOV carpool lanes, bridges and ferries — have propelled the country to the top of the electric innovators list. The incentives make electric vehicle models cheaper to buy than similar petrol models.

The results have been dramatic: In 2021, 65% of all new cars sold in Norway were electric, up from 54% in 2020 and 42% in 2019. Reuters believes that battery EVs will take 75% to 80% of the Norway market in 2022.

Christina Bu, who heads the Norwegian EV Association says, "The goal of selling only zero-emissions cars in 2025 will be within reach."

To facilitate the Nordic EV revolution, Norway currently has ten thousand publicly available charging points.

CHAPTER THREE   49

WHY SO DISRUPTIVE?

Forty percent of the average franchise dealer's profit is derived from parts and service. (Adam Simms, CEO of Price Simms Auto Group, puts that figure even higher, at as much as 60% to 80%.) The problem for dealers is that electric vehicles have significantly fewer moving parts compared with ICE vehicles. That means less to go wrong, less to repair and longer intervals between service calls.

McKinsey predicts that EVs will probably result in up to 40% less aftermarket spending when compared with similarly aged ICE vehicles.

EVs also last longer, which could lead to a drop in the frequency of new car sales.

If cars become more reliable, dealers already operating on razor-thin profit margins may plunge into the red. Many may not survive the shock.

A caveat: EVs apparently wear out their tires up to 30% faster than gasoline-powered cars due to the vehicle's increased weight and higher engine torque. The Tesla Model S weighs more than a Ford F-150, and the Ford F-150 Lightning is 35% heavier than its nonelectric counterpart, at 6,500 pounds. On-demand tire replacement service Zohr reports that its EV customers in the U.S. are coming back for tire replacements 30% more often than traditional ICE vehicle owners.

Here's a quick summary of the pros and cons for dealers:

EV IMPACT ON DEALER OPERATIONS

	Factor	Impact	Positive or Negative
EV Impact on F&I	EVs Cost More	More finance profit; more likely to sell GAP insurance	Positive
EV Impact on F&I	More Likely to Sell at MSRP	Higher front-end gross profit	Positive
EV Impact on Service & Parts	Fewer Moving Parts	Less likely to sell Vehicle Service Contracts (VSC)	Negative
EV Impact on Service & Parts	Fewer Moving Parts	Longer service intervals	Negative
EV Impact on Service & Parts	Fewer Moving Parts	McKinsey forecasts 40% less parts sales for EVs	Negative
EV Impact on Service & Parts	Tires	Increased weight and torque of EVs means more frequent tire changes	Positive

Source: Automotive Ventures

Another downside to the extra weight: safety.

In a crash between a lighter vehicle and a heavier vehicle, the passengers in the lighter vehicle are more likely to die, according to Blake Shaffer, an assistant professor in the department of economics and school of public policy at the University of Calgary. Pedestrians will be more at risk from heavier EVs.

What about PHEVs — plug-in hybrid electric cars — which have, like the Volt, a gasoline and electric engine with a cable to charge overnight? My sense is that these are just a bridge, a way for OEMs to hit EPA standards by extending the number of miles per "gallon" in the face of more restrictive emissions targets. They do help consumers get past the range anxiety of plug-in EVs. But once fast charging stations are ubiquitous and range increases, PHEVs will fade away.

Moreover, draft "green finance" regulations in Europe are taking some of the sheen off PHEVs by banning OEMs from labeling them as "sustainable investments" beyond 2025. Additional rules restricting the emission of pollutants could increase the cost of producing PHEVs.

As a result, an AutoForecast Solutions analysis of car production plans in Europe through 2028 showed only twenty-eight PHEV models versus eighty-six electric battery vehicles.

A European Commission official called its new policies "technology neutral" but added that PHEVs are now seen as "a transition technology toward zero-emission mobility."

Carlos Ghosn, the fugitive chairman and CEO of Renault and Nissan, once quipped that hybrids were like mermaids. "When you want a girl, you get a fish. When you want a fish, you get a girl."

Neither Renault nor Nissan has hybrids in its lineup, but each has an all-electric model: the Renault Zoe and the Nissan Leaf.

The move to electric would receive a boost if legislation were passed allowing owners of older gas-guzzling cars to trade them in, either for a tax credit or real money, similar to what the government did with its Cash for Clunkers program.

That program encouraged consumers to buy new cars during the recession following the housing crash of 2008 by purchasing from them their older, less fuel-efficient vehicles.

The program ended in 2009 after the $3 billion that had been allocated for it had been depleted.

EVs could be particularly welcome as part of the future of fleets.

Fleet owners' biggest expenses are depreciation (44%), fuel (22%) and maintenance and repairs (11%), according to Deloitte. Widespread adoption of EVs could slash those numbers by more than half.

And if they can be outfitted with cheap, refurbished battery packs, even high-mileage EVs may retain their value far better than gasoline-fueled cars, leading to rapid depreciation of used conventional vehicles.

STILL ROOM FOR HYDROGEN?

Toyota, for its part, isn't taking the move to EVs lying down. Despite the Prius being the original gamechanger for gasoline-electric hybrids, Toyota is now arguing *against* a 100% electric future.

Toyota executive Chris Reynolds flew to Washington, D.C., in 2021 to make the case that hybrids, rather than fully electric cars, as well as hydrogen-powered vehicles, should play a bigger role in the post-gasoline power mix.

Toyota isn't necessarily an unbiased party; the company has invested so much in the development of hydrogen fuel cells that, if 100% electric cars were to take over, it would be a blow to Toyota's bottom line.

But hydrogen doesn't seem to me to be easily commercializable. We shouldn't ignore it, but I haven't seen any reputable groups, such as McKinsey or Deloitte, claiming that hydrogen will surpass electric — at least not without some huge technological or business breakthrough. After all, Toyota's Mirai fuel-cell cars have only sold eleven thousand units since they were introduced — and that was in 2014.

At this point, all indications are that electric will be the dominant technology that gets adopted.

That seems to be the view of rival Japanese automaker Honda, which has partnered with GM to produce an electric SUV, the Prologue, to be introduced in 2024.

Honda also has killed its own hydrogen model.

"I think hydrogen holds promise but it's at least a decade behind batteries right now," notes David Friedman, vice president of advocacy at Consumer Reports and former acting administrator of the U.S. National Highway Traffic Safety Administration. "Toyota is saying, 'No, we've got to hold off; we've got to wait until they're ready with hydrogen.' But the climate can't wait."

The Honda/GM Prologue launch is part of the former company's recently announced plan to switch to zero-emissions vehicles in North America by 2040. "Our zero-emissions focus has begun," Dave Gardner, executive vice president of American Honda, said on a conference call.

Even Toyota isn't fully committing to hydrogen; the company said in April 2021 that it plans to sell fifteen electric battery models globally by 2025.

Hyundai, on the other hand, is doubling down on its hydrogen bet. A next-generation fuel-cell stack is due to be released by the company in 2023; it should slash costs by up to 50% to get closer to EV pricing, and it will be smaller, more powerful and more durable.

Hyundai is focusing first on commercial vehicles — it currently sells the Nexo crossover and the Xcient fuel-cell heavy truck. In 2023, the South Korean manufacturer will release a fuel cell-powered tractor.

Hyundai predicts that hydrogen will account for 18% of the world's energy demand by 2050, and that by popularizing hydrogen, it can help cut carbon dioxide emissions by more than six billion tons a year.

Larry Burns, GM's former corporate vice president for research, development and planning, says, "If I could change one thing in my public rhetoric in my role at GM, I probably would never have uttered the words *fuel cell*. I would have called it a 'hydrogen battery' instead, because to be honest, they're very similar."

CHAPTER THREE   53

Burns believes both electric battery-powered and hydrogen-powered cars will coexist.

"This is not battery *or* fuel cell. I think it's an *and*. Depending on which market you're dealing with, hydrogen and fuel cells are going to find their role."

RAW MATERIALS

Will trade frictions with China imperil access to the rare minerals needed in electric car batteries?

Data from Benchmark Mineral Intelligence indicates that Chinese chemical companies have considerable reach.

CHINESE CONTROL OF THE EV SUPPLY CHAIN

80%
Of the world's total output of raw materials for advanced batteries is controlled by China.

~90%
Of rare metals, alloys and magnets are under Chinese control.

8 of 14
Of the largest cobalt mines in the world are located in the Democratic Republic of Congo — and are Chinese owned.

>60%
Of the world's graphite, another essential electric battery component, is produced in China.

Source: Benchmark Mineral Intelligence

The Argonne National Laboratory in Illinois estimates that a single car's lithium-ion battery pack contains around 17 pounds of lithium, 77 pounds of nickel, 44 pounds of manganese and 30 pounds of cobalt.

A key question: Will we run out of some of these minerals, or is it more a matter of who *owns* the minerals?

A 2021 study in *Nature* suggests that current reserves of lithium should be enough to power electric vehicles through the middle of the 21st century.

"And reserves are a malleable concept," writes the study's author, Davide Castelvecchi. "For most materials, if demand goes up, reserves eventually do too."

That doesn't mean prices will stay the same. Demand for lithium is expected to increase sevenfold over the coming decade. This could result in temporary shortages and price swings, although "as more processing capacity is built, these shortages are likely to work themselves out," believes Haresh Kamath, a specialist in energy storage at the Electric Power Research Institute in Palo Alto, California.

Cobalt is a greater worry.

Two-thirds of the global supply of cobalt is mined in the Democratic Republic of the Congo, where human rights abuses, particularly child labor, remain rampant.

There's also the question of whether mining lithium and other elements used by electric batteries is any less environmentally destructive than drilling for oil. Current forms of extraction require copious amounts of energy (for lithium extracted from rock) or water (for extraction from brines).

"But more modern techniques that extract lithium from geothermal water, using geothermal energy to drive the process, are considered more benign," writes Castelvecchi. "And despite this environmental toll, mining lithium will help to displace destructive fossil fuel extraction."

CAN THE ELECTRIC GRID HANDLE AN ALL-ELECTRIC ECOSYSTEM?

"Over time, utilities will be able to support the increase in demand that EVs will put on the grid — but the key words there are 'over time,'" David Reuter, an auto industry veteran who now is chief communications officer for NextEra Energy, the nation's largest utility company and parent of Florida Power & Light Company, told *Automotive News* in January 2021.

While Reuter believes that utility companies have plenty of power and the infrastructure to charge EVs at their current growth rates, he notes that it "took many decades" to build out the U.S. gasoline and diesel fueling infrastructure. System upgrades — new transformers and the like — will be needed.

But will it be enough?

The winter of 2021's extended cold snap in Texas left many residents without power for days, raising concerns that further demands on the grid could zap the ability of overtaxed systems to respond.

New power stations — including those focused on renewable solar and wind farm energy — are now in the planning stages. As an example, a $1.6 billion, nearly 2,000-megawatt power station about 125 miles south of Cleveland will provide energy to more than a million homes in Ohio, Pennsylvania and West Virginia.

That led the U.S. Energy Information Administration to state in its 2021 *Annual Energy Outlook* report that EVs shouldn't strain the nation's electrical infrastructure if current trends hold. The agency predicts that the demand for electricity from transportation will be less than 3% of the country's total electricity needs through 2050.

Upgrades to grid infrastructure, if and when necessary, won't come cheap.

The Boston Consulting Group estimates that by 2030, an additional $1,100 investment in grid updates will be needed to support *each* battery-powered electric vehicle on the road. That's a total of $25 billion in investment if BCG's overall sales projections for EVs come to fruition.

Where will drivers plug in their EVs? By April 2021, Tesla had already installed twenty thousand of its Supercharger units globally. And, in July 2021, the company announced that it was opening the Supercharger network to non-Tesla vehicles.

"Our goal is to support the advent of sustainable energy," Musk said during an earnings call. "It's not to create a walled garden and bludgeon our competitors."

During the same call, Musk added that Tesla will soon introduce dynamic pricing, charging more for electricity at rush hour than in the middle of the night.

Utilities are already incentivizing this by dropping rates for consumers during off-peak times. Bidirectional charging — where excess power can be sold back to the grid — will help too.

Volkswagen's Krause points out that most charging will be done at home, not at a Supercharger station, using the less energy-taxing slow charge method, which can take six to seven hours to get to 100%. Most users will plug in to "replenish just 30 to 40 miles," Krause notes. "They're mostly just topping off, so I think we'll be OK."

THE FUTURE OF BATTERY TECHNOLOGY

The biggest challenge for electric vehicles has always been "range anxiety" — that's the very real fear that you could run out of juice before arriving at your destination. Whereas gasoline-powered cars can travel hundreds of miles between fill-ups, the electric car of 2007 could go no farther than about 70 miles between charges.

That's improved — up to 300 miles for the most heavily optioned Teslas, Bolts and BMWs — but it's still not as unlimited as a gasoline-powered car, for which ubiquitous gas stations make filling up as easy as flossing your teeth (if a tad more expensive).

Even as more charge spots are installed around the country, there's still the problem of time: The fastest technology today takes about forty minutes to get to an 80% charge. That's better than a six- to seven-hour overnight fueling (more typical of a Level 1 home charger), but who wants to have to stop for close to an hour on a road trip to power up — potentially several times? Consumers generally don't want to sacrifice on their driving experience by going electric.

New battery technologies are coming to address the dilemma. One of the most intriguing is from Israel's StoreDot.

StoreDot replaces the graphite used in traditional lithium-ion batteries with germanium-based nanoparticles into which ions can pass quickly and more easily. StoreDot plans to transition to silicon — which is less expensive than germanium — by 2022. In that case, the cost should be the same as existing lithium-ion batteries.

Heating graphite is what made batteries famously explode in Samsung's Galaxy Note 7.

StoreDot's batteries need a fast charging infrastructure similar to Tesla's; it's not as simple as plugging a cable into a socket in your garage. That's one reason StoreDot is working with BP, the British petroleum company.

"BP has 18,200 forecourts [service stations], and they understand that ten years from now, all these stations will be obsolete if they don't repurpose them for charging," explains StoreDot CEO Doron Myersdorf.

StoreDot demonstrated its five-minute charge on a motorcycle at the 2019 EcoMotion conference in Tel Aviv. In January 2021, the company announced that it had produced one thousand of its XFC extra-fast charging batteries, which are being distributed to electric vehicle manufacturers for testing. StoreDot is even working on electric batteries for manned and unmanned flying drones.

StoreDot's battery technology is proprietary, which might be its biggest limitation. Existing manufacturers such as Panasonic, which makes batteries for Tesla, have significant investments in their factories and methodologies; switching to a new tech won't be easy. As a result, StoreDot is planning to build its own "giga factories," primarily in China.

"We don't want to be in a situation where we have great technology but don't have the partners or the capacity to meet the demand," Myersdorf says.

StoreDot isn't alone in the ultra-fast charging business. Swiss firm ABB announced in September 2021 that its Terra 360 charging station can fully charge an EV in fifteen minutes, and it can give an additional 62 miles of range when plugged in for a mere three minutes. ABB's new charger supports up to four vehicles at once. The company has sold nearly five hundred thousand of its previous charger units. ABB is heading toward an IPO at a $3 billion valuation.

New materials may also make a difference. In addition to StoreDot's germanium-based nanoparticles, other manufacturers are exploring "silicon carbide," a mashup of silicon and carbon that can bring a 5% to 10% improvement in range.

Tesla is already on board, using silicon carbide chips supplied by STMicroelectronics NV, as is GM, which is using silicon carbide in its Ultium EV battery platform, and Toyota, for both the Prius and Toyota's hydrogen-powered Mirai.

In addition to silicon carbide, GM is also looking at another material mashup — gallium nitride — which can also boost range by up to 10%. Navitas Semiconductor claims that gallium nitride could account for up to 16% of the power semiconductor market by 2026, a huge jump from less than 1% in 2020.

ELECTRIC CHALLENGES

Electrification would seem to be an all-around net positive — for the environment and for human health — albeit less so for dealers' bottom lines. There are still some thorny questions to be resolved:

- What happens to electric car batteries when they've dropped below a minimum service level? Can they be disposed of without causing harm to the environment and to people living near the dumping sites? Can they be shifted to consumers' garages to store solar power captured during the day? For how long? Whose responsibility will that be?
- Are we just shifting the polluting parts of driving a car from city streets to the production and disposal sites, far away from the Western urban areas that will be first to adopt alternative power sources? Will a shift to 100% EVs in the West simply move the remaining ICE cars to Asia and Africa?
- How will the problem of battery degradation be solved? Today, both dealerships and consumers struggle with how to confidently purchase a used EV, given there's no real way to tell how much battery life is remaining. This lack of transparency, and its effect on EV vehicle resale values, will be compounded as

new (and better) battery technologies emerge, rendering early EV generations much less appealing to consumers.
- What retraining will be required for maintenance workers to service high-voltage powertrains safely and efficiently? What additional tools will technicians need?
- If battery technology improves, will that turn today's generation of EVs into tech dinosaurs?

MARGIN COMPRESSION AND ELECTRIC VEHICLES

During COVID-19 and the ensuing microchip shortages, both dealers and OEMs experienced record profit margins. But once supply shortages of both new and used cars return to normal, dealers will be back to an environment of margin compression.

The shift to EVs will only exacerbate that dynamic.

"Most incumbent manufacturers are selling their EVs at a loss today and for the foreseeable future until their volumes ramp up to significant numbers. How can they continue to remain profitable with this increasing pressure on traditionally thin margins?" asks Dennis Clark, former senior managing director of Honda Innovations, the innovation and corporate venture arm of Honda.

Margin compression has largely been a result of the changes to the automotive retailing landscape brought on by the internet.

Price transparency — one of those changes — hasn't been kind to dealers.

Pre-internet, dealers generally didn't disclose the invoice price on a vehicle, and consumers had no way of easily comparing costs across dealerships. Pricing transparency, perhaps more than anything else, is driving the margin out of the front end of the car deal.

It's not just the cost of the vehicle. Transparency around trade-ins, financing offers and insurance products will lead to better-armed and better-informed consumers and will further accelerate shrinking margins.

In parallel with this margin erosion, the average dealer is already struggling to keep up with the massive technology and advertising budgets of big players, such as Carvana and Lithia. It's not yet clear how or whether the average dealer is going to be able to compete with large players that have better economies of scale.

Continuing contraction in margins will need to be offset by a reduction in dealer expenses elsewhere.

"How many electric Hummers do you have to sell to make back a quarter of a million dollars" in infrastructure upgrades? asks Justin Gasman, finance director at McCaddon Cadillac Buick GMC in Boulder, Colorado. He's referring to the trend in recent years, where OEMs have been increasingly requiring dealerships that want to sell and service their vehicles to make costly upgrades with no guarantee of a quick return. "But if you don't do it, then you're further behind," Gasman adds.

"If I can make more money on an internal combustion engine vehicle, which one am I going to sell?" asks Ernie Norcross, Volvo Retail Advisory Board chairman and owner of Volvo Cars Memphis in Tennessee. "To get the network to be enthusiastic about the new electrification strategy, we should be paid as much or more."

"We need to have the dealers on board financially; otherwise, they will do whatever they can to sell combustion engines," Volvo Car USA CEO Anders Gustafsson assured worried dealers. "We will probably change the model of how we calculate things, but they will not earn less."

McKinsey estimates that EVs will only reach price parity with ICE vehicles by 2026.

It's not all doom and gloom.

"Consumers will pay less for parts but more for labor," Gustafsson believes. And the increased volume of electric battery vehicle sales will "mitigate some of the changes" related to parts and service.

Dealerships in an all-electric future may look very different than the gas-focused versions of today. "The change will be more on staffing of our dealerships, going from wrenches to a more electrical base," Jorge

Gutierrez, a corporate strategist at Bert Ogden Auto Group in Texas, told *Automotive News*. "The technician of the future may look very different from the technician of today."

CHARGING SPOTS AT THE DEALER

Where will electric car owners charge their cars? While the majority of charging will be done at the consumer's home, if EVs are to become the dominant form of transportation by 2040 and beyond, owners who don't have a dedicated parking spot or a private garage will need other options.

According to the 2019 American Housing Survey, one in three U.S. housing units does not have a garage, and many of those do not have a dedicated parking spot on the street.

Curbside charging is one solution, but "street parking has long been a lawless affair," writes Henry Grabar in *Slate*. "So far, electric vehicle charging at the curb is working much the same way: every driver for him- or herself. This raises the possibility that gas-powered cars will continue to dominate in neighborhoods with multifamily housing and the promise of cleaner air will remain unfulfilled in exactly the places that have suffered the most from the many harms of automobile exhaust."

Curbside charging also has the problem of reserving that space on the street for just one specific use — EV charging — potentially for decades, notes San Francisco MTA parking manager Hank Wilson. "Because our commercial curbs are so dynamic and changing so much, we're reticent to lock that in. It's a very expensive thing that requires a lot of infrastructure."

New York City installed its first curbside chargers in June 2021 at a cost of about $15,000 per charge spot.

Charge spots at public facilities would seem to be the logical response.

Companies like EVgo and ChargePoint have been setting up chargers in parking lots and grocery store garages; drivers without their own home chargers have been able to get by so far on this kind of infrastructure.

Do dealers have an opportunity to drive engagement by co-locating charge spots on their lots?

If EV owners have to come to the dealer for their forty-minute charges (and maybe a car wash and cleaning thrown in while they're there), what other products and services could dealers upsell while they have a captive, charging audience?

Alternatively, could dealers get into the business of installing home charge spots, in the same way that buying a dishwasher at Home Depot includes installation? First-time EV buyers are not familiar with the intricacies of charge spot manufacturers, different wattage levels, fast versus slow charge, etc. Dealers could provide a value-added service, which they may (or choose not to) charge for.

Monthly maintenance contracts (think AppleCare for EVs) that would cover fixes to your home charger as needed (or removing it if you are no longer driving electric) could become another revenue source for dealers.

Dealers will need to address many questions for their customers:

- 🚗 Which chargers are best?
- 🚗 Do I need different adapters for different types of vehicles?
- 🚗 Do I visit a consumer's home *before* a purchase to make sure they've got the right charger installed or the necessary infrastructure to support home charging?

New technologies may make charging even easier.

Hyundai announced in 2021 that its Genesis GV60 luxury compact SUV will be its first 100% EV with a wireless charging option. Instead of a plug, drivers simply position their vehicle over a charging pad. A full charge will take six hours. While that's not as fast as a Tesla Supercharger, it does mean you can never claim, when arriving late for a meeting or party, that you forgot to plug in.

Another promising wireless charging option involves burying electrified wire coils in the concrete bed of a highway to create a magnetic field along the road surface. (Think iPhone MagSafe but for cars . . . while they're driving!)

In order to use these roads, cars would need to be fitted with a receiver coil to pick up the charge from the embedded coils. The Indiana Department of Transportation was one of the first to give it a try: The state contracted with the German firm Magment to implement the test.

Another German firm, the giant Siemens, is building a "scaffolding" of cables and wires above a 3-mile stretch of road outside Frankfurt that will allow cars to charge as they drive, similar to the city's trams.

Volkswagen and the Israeli startup Electreon have rolled out their own in-road charging prototype on a highway between the Italian cities of Brescia and Milan, on a 2.5-kilometer stretch of highway in Sweden, as well as on a 2-kilometer stretch in northern Tel Aviv. The layer of asphalt eliminates the chances of passersby getting electrocuted, Electreon CEO Oren Ezer told *Bloomberg Businessweek*.

Khurram Afridi, an associate professor of electrical and computer engineering at Cornell University, described how the different charging technologies would work.

"Highways would have a charging lane, sort of like a high-occupancy lane," Afridi told Business Insider. "If you were running out of battery, you would move into the charging lane. It would be able to identify which car went into the lane, and it would later send you a bill."

The need is certainly there. A recent study from University of California, Davis, found that one in five electric car owners switched back to a gasoline-powered car due to the hassle of needing to find an EV charging station.

"Charging is an incredible sitting-duck opportunity for retail," Reilly Brennan, general partner at Trucks VC, told me.

THE TIPPING POINT

"The dam is breaking; the tipping point is here," says Sam Ricketts, a member of the team that authored Washington Gov. Jay Inslee's climate action plan during his 2020 presidential run.

The trend is impossible to miss.

More than seven million electrified vehicles are currently traversing the world's streets, including one million Teslas and a half million BMWs. North American car manufacturers plan to triple the number of non-gasoline-powered models by 2024.

"Something has tipped," says Burns. "That something is money. Electric cars are easier to build because they are less complex and have far fewer parts."

It won't be immediate; there are still roughly 1.5 billion gasoline-powered cars and trucks out there. Moreover, there are fewer public fast charging stations across the U.S. than there are gas stations in the state of Alabama alone.

In the meantime, expect to see electric delivery vans from Amazon pulling up to your driveway. The e-commerce giant agreed in 2019 to purchase one hundred thousand electric vehicles from startup Rivian, as part of an ambitious push to make Amazon's fleet run entirely on renewable energy.

Rivian is more than the recipient of a good deal from Amazon; the partnership also helped Rivian raise more than $10 billion in venture capital money and have a very successful IPO near the end of 2021, quickly surpassing Ford's and GM's market cap.

Amazon has invested around $700 million in Rivian, as part of its $2 billion Climate Pledge Fund. After Rivian's IPO, Amazon owned more than 20% of the company, with a value of more than $20 billion.

Tesla's market cap of $1.1 trillion makes it the sixth most valuable company on the planet.

"Electrifying transportation is our future,'" says Kristin Dziczek, an economist with Ann Arbor, Michigan's Center for Automotive Research. "That train has left the station. We're on that path."

CHAPTER FOUR

VEHICLE PRODUCTION

"We are really committed to going to an order-based system and keeping incentives at fifty to sixty days' supply. I know we are wasting our money on incentives."
— *Jim Farley, CEO of Ford*

In the 1970s, Toyota adopted a system of "Just-in-Time" manufacturing. Also known as the Toyota Production System, it was a management strategy that aligned orders of automotive parts with assembly-line schedules so that goods are received only when needed, reducing inventory costs and decreasing waste.

Just-in-Time manufacturing has, in the half century since Toyota popularized it, become the de facto methodology for smart companies striving to take advantage of the economies of scale that international sourcing of components provide. (It has also demonstrated the precarious interconnectedness of the global supply chain — something that became apparent during the COVID-19 crisis, when lockdowns led to a slowdown in semiconductor production, which severely impacted manufacturing timelines in automotive and beyond.)

Notwithstanding the chip shortage, the Just-in-Time model is poised to make another leap — and this time, not just to streamline internal manufacturing efficiencies, but also to enable OEMs to migrate a much larger proportion of their production to "built to order," assembling only the cars consumers have bought or ordered. The art will be to do that quickly enough that consumers need not wait weeks or longer for a new car to roll off the assembly line.

Think of it as the Amazonification of car manufacturing: near instant gratification powered by precise marketing and data.

Now, compare that with the way most car manufacturing is done today.

A planner in Detroit, Japan or Munich decides, for example, that the U.S. can absorb ten thousand red Camaros or Camrys in the next month. The forecasting in this scenario is still largely top down, along the lines of "We will build what we think the market can absorb."

If the forecast is off, then consumers will be offered all manner of discounts to purchase vehicles they don't necessarily want but might be inclined to settle for if the incentive is high enough. The average manufacturer incentive in 2021 was $2,065 per vehicle. Before COVID-19, the average manufacturer incentive hovered at about 10% of MSRP, or about $4,000 per new vehicle sold. OEMs spend an estimated $30 billion to $50 billion a year in incentives.

That's a lose-lose as far as the big picture goes.

It leads to disgruntled dealers, who are making less and sitting on more inventory than they would have if the car-to-consumer match were more accurate, as well as unhappy customers, who had their hearts set on a navy-blue Kia Sportage but wound up receiving a red one (although a well-executed incentive could turn red into the new blue).

This convoluted situation made a certain amount of sense before the internet. What else could you do, after all, when it was impossible to measure consumer demand in real time? So planners would ask themselves, mostly in the dark:

- "How many vehicles did we sell last year?"
- "Can we increase that by 10% this year with our new, sexier model?"
- "Did white sell better than black in 2020?"
- "Can we use similar heuristics to decide on features for 2022?"

Nowadays, consumers want total choice over color, trim, features, engine size, CarPlay or Android Auto and more. And yet, decisions made before a car even hits production are based on the crudest of data, without consumer demand playing much of a part.

In Europe, a Just-in-Time system *is* in place, but it hasn't made car buyers any happier.

You order your new BMW in Cologne; then you have to wait several weeks (or more) for it to be manufactured in Munich and shipped to the closest dealer. You can't just drive off the lot with the car you want — unless you're willing to travel hundreds of miles to a dealer that has the car in the right color and trim.

Americans, meanwhile, are not willing to wait for their customized cars. They're not willing to wait for *anything* in today's convenience economy, for that matter, not when you can have a tub of double-fudge chocolate-mocha ice cream delivered to your house in fifteen minutes (quite literally . . . I tried it).

So how do you tell an excited (and impatient) in-market car buyer, "Sorry, you'll have to wait several weeks for your car to be ready"?

Well, actually, you *can* say that — if you're a premium brand like Tesla.

You won't find a big parking lot in front of your local Tesla mall location with a bunch of prebuilt vehicles you can test-drive and leave with the same day. You order and then wait anywhere from two to six months.

CHAPTER FOUR   69

Tesla buyers accept the inconvenience because of the aura that they're getting exactly the car they want (and because Tesla is perceived as a sexy status symbol). But this is more of an edge case. It's not the same motivation as, "Hey, my car died, and I need a new Camry *right now!*"

Still, the holy grail is the same. If manufacturers knew what their customers wanted, they could save billions of dollars on incentives they are forced to deploy when the wrong vehicles are built or the right vehicles are shipped to the wrong location.

- Is Denver in January really the best place to send two truckloads of Corvettes?
- How much will an OEM or dealer have to spend to ship those unwanted convertibles from Denver to Miami?

But if manufacturers could better identify what to build, when and where, it could help boost their financial health.

The same goes for dealers:

- No more glut of purple Mustangs being peddled in California with a $2,000 discount because purple was fashionable in 2020, but by 2022 . . . not so much.
- No heated headlights in Miami or four-wheel-drive BMWs in Atlanta when where they're really needed is in New Hampshire or North Dakota.

Indeed, if OEMs had perfect visibility into consumer demand and could optimize the supply chain, buyers would get the car they want, dealers would maximize profitability (without resorting to discounting) and OEMs could ship the right cars to the right geographies with no incentives required.

Reducing the footprint of dealer parking lots would lead to more profit all around — less rent required for real estate, less "floorplan expense" and fewer cars overproduced by the OEMs.

Eliminating dealer floorplan expenses is part of Volvo's road map.

"We will see more pull and less push in the future; that's good for our margins," says Volvo CEO Håkan Samuelsson. "You will see more deliver-to-order [although] customers may need to wait some more days for their car." Volvo's post-COVID-19 "new normal" will focus on lower sales volumes with higher margins.

Doug Betts, president of J.D. Power's automotive division, notes that "88% of [a manufacturer's] configurations sell fewer than fifty units each" — what Betts calls automotive "unicorns" (not the same as the tech world's use of the term to describe a company with a billion-dollar valuation) — and that "these configurations account only for 25% of its total sales."

For this, Brian Finkelmeyer, senior director of New Car Solutions at Cox Automotive-owned vAuto, has a simple solution: "Dealers need to focus on the 12% of combinations that make up 75% of the sales," he writes on the WardsAuto website.

But how to do that?

SOFTWARE TO THE RESCUE

Software may be able to bridge some of the gap by providing manufacturers with the data they need to make smarter decisions.

J.D. Power's Helix is a good example.

The configuration analysis platform fuses together 4.5 billion data points from two main areas: content (features such as sunroofs, leather interiors and adaptive cruise control) and sales performance data (days to turn, vehicle gross, vehicle price).

This kind of access to highly precise vehicle configuration intelligence enables manufacturers to "identify equipment in advance that doesn't enhance profitability, generate volume or drive compliance," the company's sales literature states.

Where will the data come from?

Some will be taken from dealers' sales records and from dealer management systems. The tech giants — Google, Facebook and Amazon — could easily start to provide data to the OEMs, as well.

This might include the following:

- Which vehicle-related terms are being searched?
- What are people searching for, at what price, and in what locations? Do Texans prefer built-in baby seats? Do New Yorkers opt for collision avoidance systems?
- How many "likes" is a particular vehicle getting on social media?
- How long are users "hovering" over a sponsored ad?
- What are car buyers searching for when they look not at your site or the vehicles you offer, but at your *competition*?

Manufacturers can do some level of this kind of data analysis themselves. Sifting through Google searches is time-consuming, however, and the search data may not be as transparently available as it was a decade before. Silicon Valley would be happy to wrap that data up with a nice bow and provide it to the OEMs — for a price, of course.

Google is already experimenting with including vehicle detail pages and inventory within the search interface rather than presenting standard links that send searchers off to a third-party automotive site. Google's vehicle listings also show the most searched-for options for a particular car. (While this feature first appeared in April 2021, it has since been removed. Visiting http://google.com/local/cars currently results in a 404 error, although I expect the page to return at some point soon.)

If Google does, in fact, decide to keep this feature and not relegate it to the status of back-burner experiment, dealers may have no choice but to play ball and pay Google to list their inventory and, presumably, get data insights in return as part of the deal. That could be enticing enough to convince manufacturers and dealers to reallocate more of their ad spend away from third-party automotive marketplaces and onto Google.

That said, even if GM went to Google and asked for real-time information on preferred Corvette colors, and even if Google were so generous as to share that data (perhaps even without compensation), GM might not have the technology today to act on it.

The alternative, though, is a dead end as we barrel into the future. Without data, you might see a lot of red Corvettes out there, but that doesn't necessarily mean there's a lot of demand.

3D-PRINT A CAR?

Today, some car parts can be 3D-printed on-demand at a local dealer or repair facility. In the future, could an entire car be printed? This could change the economics of car manufacturing entirely, moving production from a centralized facility to a regional one — or even to your own garage.

Now-defunct Phoenix-based Local Motors showed off its plans to 3D-print a vehicle at the 2015 North American International Auto Show. Local Motors' vehicle demo was constructed from a carbon-polymer composite. Workers still needed to install the vehicle's motor, suspension and tires manually.

"We like to think of it as Build-A-Bear, mashed up with Ikea, mashed up with Formula One," CEO John B. Rogers Jr. jokingly told the *New York Times* at the time. In a video made with late-night television host James Corden, Rogers dubbed his company's vehicles "bespoke."

Local Motors has since focused its attention on Olli, a 3D-printed autonomous electric shuttle. It took about ten hours to print an Olli. Another Local Motors car, the Strati, a convertible dune buggy, took some forty-four hours to print.

While printing a complete VW Jetta at home might be a stretch, we could very well see small production plants in every neighborhood, where the cars or their parts could be printed.

Not so fast, says Dave Paratore, former CEO of advanced materials maker NanoSteel.

"Regional production is going to be hard to do," he told me. "We produce seventeen million new cars per year that need to be defect-free.

From a consistency standpoint, parts and inputs on the production line need to be very closely controlled. So it's very hard to regionalize production. You could regionalize assembly, but you would need robots, which are expensive."

Simplified car design will help propel 3D printing.

An Israeli startup, REE, has developed a lightweight, modular electric vehicle chassis, where the car's major components — brakes, thermal systems, motor and drivetrain — are situated next to the wheels. Looking a little like a high-tech skateboard, REE's platform can be used for multiple types of vehicles — from a high-performance car able to do 0 to 60 mph in under three seconds to a 10-ton truck.

"The design and validation of each platform traditionally costs manufacturers billions of dollars," REE CEO Daniel Barel says. By reusing the same design, the cost savings should be substantial. REE is collaborating with Mitsubishi and some as-yet-unnamed Chinese OEMs.

3D-printing technology may not be fully baked for another twenty to thirty years. It's easier to 3D-print with polymers than with metal. And, clearly, it's easier to 3D-print a new dashboard than an electric battery.

But the ultimate in Just-in-Time manufacturing is coming, and it behooves all of us in the automotive retail space to follow the technology carefully.

ONGOING IMPACT OF THE CHIP SHORTAGE

COVID-19 created an unexpected reality for automotive manufacturers: a global chip shortage. It resulted from a perfect storm of temporarily lessened demand for new vehicles (when many people were locked down at home), coupled with increased interest in consumer electronics, which began to boom even more than usual in the new, if temporary, reality of sheltering in place.

When OEMs saw, at the beginning of the pandemic, that consumers were buying fewer vehicles, they cut orders, prompting chipmakers to shift their attention to other industries. So, when demand for vehicles returned by late 2020, the chips they needed were already allocated elsewhere. (The consumer electronics business felt the pinch too.)

Consulting firm AlixPartners estimates that the chip shortage will cost the industry $210 billion while reducing production of new vehicles by 7.7 million in 2021.

The shortage is expected to continue through 2023.

Semiconductors have long since evolved from a "nice to have" for the most advanced vehicles. Today's cars are, more than ever, a "computer on wheels" — more electronic than mechanical, with between one thousand and three thousand chips per vehicle.

Intel CEO Pat Gelsinger says that, by 2030, chips will make up 20% of the components of premium cars — five times more than their proportion in 2019.

Electric vehicles will only exacerbate the need for more and better chips.

It's not an easy problem to solve. Automotive manufacturers can't exactly build their own semiconductor factories, like Apple is doing, although Tesla appears to be doing just that. The company's D1 is a custom AI chip for training the machine-learning algorithm that powers Tesla's Autopilot.

Huei Peng, a professor at the University of Michigan who focuses on autonomous driving, says if the D1 proves successful, Tesla CEO Elon Musk conceivably could sell it to other carmakers.

Still, "it's not like you can just build a plant in thirty days. It takes roughly about 2.5 years," Patrick Penfield, a supply chain management professor at Syracuse University, told Recode.

The chip shortage has led to some significant real-world implications.

In August 2021, in response to the chip shortage, Toyota announced it was slashing the number of cars it would manufacture by 40%. In the same year, GM idled its plant that produces the Chevy Bolt, while Nissan shuttered an assembly plant in Tennessee.

CHAPTER FOUR

Other manufacturers have stripped out premium features that rely on electronics:

- GM has sold some of its newest pickups and SUVs without advanced gas management systems or wireless charging features.
- Nissan left navigation systems out of thousands of vehicles.
- Musk noted that Tesla has seen "insane difficulties" with its supply chain since the onset of COVID-19.

"The inventory shortage is changing the way we sell cars," Cliff Banks, automotive industry analyst and editor of the *Banks Report,* told me.

What might that look like?

"OEMs may back off incentives," Banks proposes. "Historically, they go back to this, but this may be a different world today. And more competitors are coming in. Manufacturers need to be open to using this opportunity. Maybe this gives them the chance to restructure their plants. We'll see."

Indeed, incentives are not what they used to be.

That 2021 figure for new vehicle incentives of $2,065 per vehicle was actually down significantly — by $2,170 a car — from a year prior due to increased demand as a result of chip-related vehicle shortages.

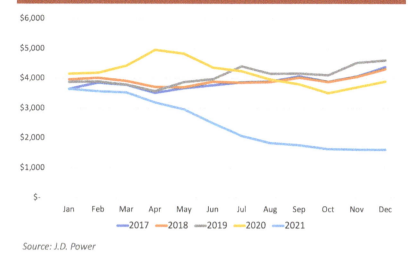

Source: J.D. Power

Expressed as a percentage of MSRP, that's just 4.8% of the total, the first time that incentives have dropped below 5%. While not great for consumers, the savings flows directly to the bottom line of OEM's P&L statements.

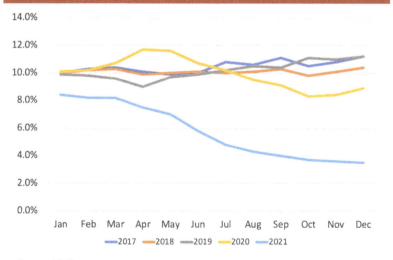

Source: J.D. Power

CHAPTER FOUR

Banks adds that if he were an OEM or a dealer today, "I'd be looking to retrain customers away from a negotiation mentality to one of 'This is the price.'" That said, "there will always be some dealers who go back to undercutting on price" using incentives and discounts.

The bottom line, emphasizes Banks: "If you can't get inventory, you can't sell cars. So dealers are going to have to get really creative."

OEMS VERSUS DEALERS

From the very beginning, OEMs and dealers have had a fraught relationship. In the U.S., OEMs generally are prohibited from selling direct to consumers. And, as I noted in Chapter Two, many believe that's a good thing.

Cars are a "highly complex mechanical product," I quoted former GM chairman Alfred Sloan as saying, and so it makes sense that consumers will "depend on their dealers to service and maintain the product for them."

The legacy automakers have tried, and failed, in the past to structure direct-to-consumer sales channels. Time and time again, attempts have proven that OEMs struggle in operating according to a retail model. So far, retail operations have best been left in the hands of the dealers.

But the new generation of OEMs are pushing the boundaries.

Tesla, notably, has been going state by state litigating in a concerted effort to revamp or strike down laws prohibiting manufacturers from selling direct to consumers.

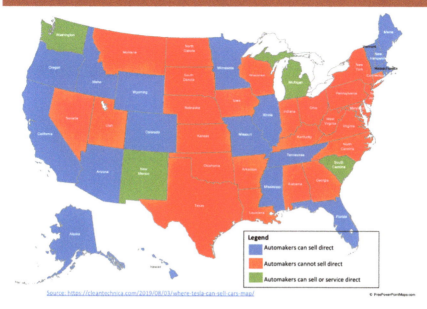

It's succeeded already in the states of New Hampshire, Minnesota, Washington, Massachusetts, Missouri, Wyoming, Arizona, Indiana, Rhode Island, Utah, Michigan and Colorado.

In another eight states — Virginia, Ohio, New Jersey, Maryland, Pennsylvania, New York, Georgia and North Carolina — Tesla has been granted permission to open a limited number of stores (between three and six dealerships).

In New Mexico, Tesla has figured out how to get around laws preventing it from selling direct to consumer: The company has opened a facility in a defunct casino on Nambé Pueblo tribal land north of Santa Fe, where state law does not apply.

Michigan — home to the headquarters of some of the most storied automotive companies in the U.S. — acceded in 2020 to allow Tesla to sell and service cars in the state, but, in a convoluted arrangement, the cars must be titled outside the state and transferred to a new Michigan title after purchase. Further, Tesla may not own a service center directly in Michigan (although a wholly owned subsidiary can).

Tesla's argument is that it shouldn't be beholden to laws prohibiting OEMs from usurping dealers, because Tesla doesn't have a franchise dealer model in the first place.

If Tesla can sell direct to the consumer, however, other OEMs may want "in" on the action — and fast. After all, how can you compete with Tesla if they control the entire consumer experience, manage the supply chain better and, as a result, presumably generate greater profits?

This will be particularly relevant for brand-new EV manufacturers such as Fisker and Rivian, which, like Tesla, don't have a dealer network, although as Jay Vijayan, CEO of automotive cloud technology company Tekion, told me, "While newer companies may try to emulate Tesla stores, it's tough to do that at scale."

Rivian is now able to sell its R1T pickup truck and R1S SUV direct to consumers from stores in the states where Tesla has blazed a path.

Is it any wonder dealers are anxious?

The rise of digital tools could shift more of the sales process to the OEMs.

"The line between automaker and retailer threatens to get blurrier as the two sides wrangle over those tools and customer data," writes Laurence Iliff in *Automotive News*.

"What we're talking about here is the OEMs exerting more control over the retail process and the retail customer experience," adds Peter Lanzavecchia, owner of Burns Buick GMC, Burns Hyundai, and Genesis of Cherry Hill in New Jersey. "We sometimes get the feeling from some of the legacy OEMs that they wish they could bring their [new EV lines] to market as a sub-brand through a distribution channel."

Nevertheless, Lanzavecchia cautions against thinking in terms of "conspiracy theories [such as] 'Is this good for us? Is it only good for them?'"

Direct-to-consumer is clearly good for the OEMs, and it's pretty good for consumers too, especially if prices drop. Indeed, it's good for just about everyone — except the dealers, of course. That's why the dealer response has been to conduct intense lobbying to keep intact anachronistic franchise laws.

OEMs don't have a great track record of trying to go direct-to-consumer.

Many automakers had factory-owned retail stores in Europe, but that experiment largely failed.

In 1997, General Motors announced plans to acquire eleven or twelve poorly performing locations and consolidate them into four or five larger stores. They quickly realized that they didn't have a competency in turning around retail locations.

In 1998, Ford planned to acquire and run retail locations in up to thirty markets and started by acquiring existing dealerships in Tulsa, Oklahoma City, Salt Lake City and Rochester, New York. The initiative, named "The Auto Collections," was initially meant to counter dealership consolidation and prepare for the evolution of the internet. But Ford ended the experiment after just three years.

Ford not only dramatically lost market share in these stores, but they also created a lot of relationship damage with the other Ford dealerships in these markets.

As for Tesla, former AutoNation CEO Mike Jackson thinks the electric vehicle company is moving too quickly.

They "didn't build a customer care network to take care of [repairs]. So we hear every day from Tesla customers who are fed up with the amount of time it takes for their cars to be cared for," Jackson told Adam Jonas, managing director of Morgan Stanley's research division.

Jackson points out that hybrid arrangements, where OEMs take reservations online and then send the customer to a dealer, "haven't had much added value for consumers. At the end of the day, everything gets transferred over to us, and you can't even specify your vehicle in this reservation."

Jackson might have been thinking about GM's Hummer.com, where you pick the car you want and order it online. Then it's delivered to a dealer (you get to choose which, and the dealer gets some of the profit).

While that sounds like a good deal for both OEM and dealer, it prevents the dealer from influencing the consumer in the purchase process. If the dealer is just a "dumb" point of delivery, it loses the opportunity to forge a long-lasting relationship with buyers, not to mention to score a few short-term upsells.

But the concept of "creating new car lines that are slightly different than what the dealers are getting will continue," says Tony Rimas, president of Dallas-based Repairify.

That might be one way OEMs and dealers will be able to coexist selling the same brand. It's similar to the way consumer electronics manufacturers offer "online only" sales and unique configurations with their own SKU numbers to differentiate them from what's offered in a brick-and-mortar store.

Lanzavecchia, who signed up for the Hummer program, told *Automotive News* that strong demand for big EVs like the Hummer lends itself to a nontraditional approach to inventory management, if only because the vehicles coming to the dealership are going first to customers on a waiting list.

The dance between OEM and dealer gets murkier when we consider that OEMs haven't always had the best track record for building software.

Venture capitalist Reilly Brennan recalls GM's BuyPower, that was meant to create "a wonderful software experience around dealerships." GM invested $15 million into the project, which allowed buyers to shop from a centralized GM portal loaded with a million new and preowned GM vehicles. Buyers would configure their ride online, then choose a nearby dealer for pickup.

The BuyPower.com site launched in 1999 as a lead-generation tool for dealers. By 2001, 88% of GM's 6,700 U.S. dealers had signed up.

"Traditional manufacturers had isolated themselves behind retailers, and we thought it was important to find a way to form direct relationships with our end consumers," said Dan McNicholl, GM North America's CIO for Information Systems and Service in 2001.

But the program was "dicey," adds Ann Blakney, the GM director responsible for the nationwide launch of BuyPower.com. "They had to accept a new way of selling, which included sending potential buyers an email price quote."

That was revolutionary in 1999.

And yet, today, "Do we still talk about BuyPower?" questions Brennan. Certainly not in the same way. GM BuyPower has morphed into something much more prosaic: Instead of sophisticated software, BuyPower is now a credit card backed by Capital One.

"Over time, OEMs have not proven to be great when it comes to building software for retail," Brennan notes wryly.

TAKE CARE WITH "CARE BY VOLVO"

In 2017, Volvo launched a program called Care by Volvo that aimed to sell subscriptions for new vehicles direct to consumers.

The program, offered via the company's website, started off by promoting the newly released Volvo XC40 compact SUV. It ran into dealer-versus-OEM problems when Volvo franchise dealerships in California complained that they were being forced to sign an amendment to their dealer agreement, making them "limited agents" of Volvo. Only then could they complete the Care by Volvo subscriptions.

In response, in 2019, the California New Car Dealers Association (CNCDA) filed a petition with the state's New Motor Vehicle Board contending that Volvo was undermining "the traditional role of Volvo dealer franchisees" and that the addendum Volvo dealers were forced to sign was "unlawful," violating several provisions of the California Vehicle Code.

Most damagingly, the CNCDA said that Care by Volvo was not really a subscription, but a marketing ploy — a two-year lease in disguise.

In February 2020, the California Department of Motor Vehicles released a scathing report upholding the CNCDA's claims. Volvo could not sell XC40 subscriptions direct to consumers from its website at the same time as the XC40 was also for sale in dealerships without a subscription, the DMV concluded.

"This constituted Volvo competing with the dealers from inside each dealership," the DMV report found.

Even worse, if a Volvo dealer didn't agree to sign the addendum (it was, after all, ostensibly optional), Volvo could be guilty of "discriminating in favor of [Volvo's] factory [owned stores and] against any dealership that did not participate."

Volvo terminated Care by Volvo in the summer of 2020 and began working on a version 2.0, which is today offered across the U.S. except in California, Hawaii, Mississippi, North Carolina, North and South Dakota and New York.

No other states filed similar petitions against Volvo for its subscription program.

Meanwhile, Volvo announced that it will switch to a "central stock" model for its new electric vehicles, in which the automaker will carry inventory on its balance sheet and deliver customer-ordered cars to dealerships.

UPGRADE OR DOWNSIZE?

There's also pressure of a different kind on dealers from OEMs: to spend a ton to upgrade their showrooms.

"We're not [going] after dealer profitability," Mercedes-Benz USA boss Dimitris Psillakis stressed to *Automotive News*. "We want to offer more product under the same scheme."

Yet it's exactly that scheme that is bleeding some dealers dry.

Volvo estimates upgrades to a dealer's infrastructure could range between $50,000 and $300,000 per store; GM has asked its Cadillac and GMC dealers who plan to sell electric vehicles to invest $200,000 in their facilities on average.

"The OEMs are pushing dealers for bigger and more luxurious facilities," Andrew Walser, CEO of Walser Automotive Group and chairman of FUSE Autotech, told me. "That's contradictory to what they're telling us about e-commerce. I hear from every OEM about doorway delivery, but then they want us to have this $10 million facility."

Ed French agrees.

"OEMs want these beautiful Taj Mahals for dealers," the automotive industry consultant explains. "But then they say, 'We don't want the consumer coming in. We want them to have a great driveway experience.' Do we really need a $10 million showroom improved every five years? Or is smaller better?"

When Andrew Gordon, who founded DealerScience (which he sold to TrueCar in 2018 for $27 million), was working in his family's Honda dealership, Honda demanded they put $1 million into their store.

"How is this kind of investment going to help us sell more cars or make more money?" he wondered.

Moreover, some of Honda's requirements simply didn't make sense.

"Honda told us that we needed to add more storage for parts," Gordon recalls. "However, our parts room had plenty of room to stock all of the parts we needed. If we can fit all of the parts that we need in the current room we have, why do we need to add empty space? In order to meet the minimum requirements for a Honda-compliant showroom, we needed to add the space whether we used it or not."

I recall visiting a Porsche dealership in San Diego. They were in the midst of a Porsche-mandated update. I asked them how it was going.

"We're frustrated," the manager told me. "Porsche has specific tile and paint vendors that you have to use. They wanted to charge us $100 per square meter for tiles. I looked at tile samples and found the exact same ones and someone local to install it for less. We did that, but when Porsche came to the store, they told us we had to rip it all out. It wasn't to their specification. I argued with them, 'It's exactly the same tile.' 'No,' they responded. 'You have to have one of *our* installers put it in.'"

The tension will only grow as companies such as Carvana (which today only sells used cars), Lithia and someday even Amazon begin to sell new cars online and with national delivery.

In that case, if you live in Boston but the new Mercedes you want is in Atlanta, no problem; they'll just ship it to you. How would a Mercedes dealership in Boston react to that — especially after their OEM just forced them to spend several million dollars on a major facility improvement, and yet that same dealer is now losing sales because an out-of-state dealer is able to sell in their territory?

What's good for the customer will very likely result in unhappy dealerships. Or as Chase Fraser, a partner with FM Capital, told me, "Dealers are about to revolt."

When an industry is in as much flux as automotive retailing, it's time to think out of the box.

What if OEMs, dealers, third-party vendors and even classified advertising sites agreed to lay down their competitive armor and share the data they have? That could, counterintuitively, make everyone *more* competitive in a rapidly changing world.

Dealers feel they have control over their data, but they don't. The same is true for pretty much everyone throughout the industry.

But if COVID-19 and microchip shortages have taught us anything, there is a future in which dealers and OEMs don't have to discount cars because the right cars are being built, and they're being shipped into the right geographies for the right customers. Cars will sell more quickly, at a higher profit, and consumers will leave happier.

It's easy to fall back on old patterns of overproduction and tension between players. The industry can and must do better if it wishes to thrive.

CHAPTER FIVE

VEHICLE OWNERSHIP

"When there's no other dude in the car, the cost of taking an Uber anywhere becomes cheaper than owning a vehicle. So the magic there is, you basically bring the cost below the cost for ownership for everybody, and then car ownership goes away."
— Travis Kalanick, former CEO of Uber

In the last few years, more than one hundred car subscription services have sprung up around the world. Companies such as Fair, Autonomy/NextCar, Drover, Clutch, Faaren, Bipi, Carro, ViveLaCar, Carvolution, CarPlanner, FreshCar and Borrow are all pushing subscription models.

"I don't think people will be owning their cars like we do today," says former GM exec Larry Burns. "I expect it will be more like a lease or subscription. I think about it through the lens of my two daughters, who are 30 and 27. My coming-of-age was when I got my driver's license and my first car. Their coming-of-age was their first cellphone, not their first car."

Burns adds that, over the last ten or fifteen years, he's asked his daughters what they would give up first, their cell phone or their car. "And they say they'd give up the car before they'd give up their handheld device. Younger generations are expressing themselves in a much different way than just through car ownership."

Burns was responding to a question from Derek Pankratz for *Deloitte Insights Magazine*. (Burns also had a lot to say about autonomous vehicles, the subject of his book *Autonomy: The Quest to Build the Driverless Car – and How It Will Reshape Our World*. More on that in Chapter Six.)

While a generational shift in car ownership may be underway, vehicle subscription adoption has been slow going so far — indeed, some would say that the subscription model has already failed — but well-funded companies continue to try to innovate in this area.

If a successful subscription model eventually emerges, ownership may very well shift away from individual consumers to fleets (OEMs, rental car agencies), with the norm becoming monthly fees instead of the traditional down payment and loan. The promise is that consumers will save money and OEMs will be able to take advantage of a whole range of new business models and revenue upsells.

Subscriptions could be equally impactful — although not necessarily in a good way — for the average dealership if it's unable (or unwilling) to participate in the subscription model. After all, if I am not buying my own car, why do I need to establish a relationship with a dealer?

Scott Painter, CEO of subscription car-as-a-service vendor Autonomy (the rebranded NextCar) and the founder of subscription car service Fair, cites a study by McKinsey predicting that, by 2025, at least 20% of all new and used car retail sales will be in the form of a subscription.

"Vehicle subscription is an antidote to the affordability concerns and economic uncertainty faced by today's car shopper," Painter says. Car subscription was "an attractive value proposition for consumers before the pandemic [that] is even more compelling today."

A 2019 survey by strategic consultancy Capgemini found that one-third of consumers would prefer a subscription model over traditional vehicle ownership. For electric vehicles in Europe, that number jumps to 50%, Capgemini reports.

Clutch Technologies, which provides back-end tools to help dealers, OEMs and fleet operators offer vehicles by subscription and is owned by Cox Automotive in the U.S., surveyed its customers in 2019. It found that 40% of consumers said that, while transportation is necessary, owning a vehicle is not. Seventy percent of surveyed customers indicated they would be interested in a vehicle subscription service.

HOW DO SUBSCRIPTIONS WORK?

A car subscription is similar to a long-term rental or a short-term lease.

"If we just call them leases, then they're already pretty popular," Reilly Brennan of Trucks VC says.

All the car subscription services I'm tracking offer a range of features for one all-inclusive monthly fee. This typically includes both major repairs and routine maintenance, insurance, taxes, licensing and registration. Some companies, like Bipi in Spain, will even arrange to pay any traffic fines for you. Drivers are responsible for their own gas, and subscription packages often have mileage limits (only a few companies offer an all-you-can-drive option).

Clutch Technologies describes two models for vehicle subscriptions:

- On-demand rentals. Based on the existing rental model, Clutch's software "simplifies the car rental process with in-app bookings and more flexible terms," and it can help "monetize idle loaner [cars] and preowned vehicles."
- Single vehicle subscriptions. This is what we're mostly addressing in this chapter, where customers gain "freedom of access

[without] the responsibility of ownership." For dealers and OEMs, this generates a "margin-rich recurring revenue stream," Clutch says.

Despite the initial buzz and many hundreds of millions of dollars raised, however, none of the current crop of subscription services has gained substantial market share or taken much of a dent out of traditional automotive sales.

The most dramatic example is that of Fair, which was forced to hit the brakes in 2019 when SoftBank, its lead investor, got cold feet about injecting more money into the company. CEO Painter stepped down, 40% of Fair's staff was laid off and downloads of its consumer app were suspended.

The biggest problem with the subscription model is that the greatest value proposition to consumers just doesn't seem to resonate: the option to change vehicles easily and frequently, with minimum periods as brief as just a month.

The idea would seem simple and appealing: Pick up a sturdy sedan for commuting in winter, then swap it for a sporty 4x4 for summer outings. Best of all, according to this model, you can cancel whenever you wish.

The Würzburg, Germany-based car subscription service Faaren proudly proclaims on its website, "A convertible in summer and an SUV in winter — drive what and when you want." Cancellation requires just twenty-one days' advance notice.

ViveLaCar, also based in Germany, has a three-month cancellation policy.

"Drive your car for as long as you want. If it no longer suits you, simply give it back or find a new one," the company's website reads.

The reality is a bit different.

"Most drivers are not changing that often," Faaren CPO Maximilian Renoth told the *AIM Group Marketplaces Report*. "They're keeping their car on average for ten to eighteen months."

At ViveLaCar, drivers rarely swap before ten months.

Madrid-based Bipi is experiencing much the same thing.

"Only 3% [of our customers] want to swap more frequently" than every couple of years, says Bipi CEO Hans Christ. Why?

"It's a pain to change cars."

And at Singapore-based Carro, even though customers can change vehicles after a month (for used cars) and every six months (for new ones), "they are reluctant to do so," explains Aaron Tan, the company's CEO.

What *is* proving attractive to consumers is the bundle business, meaning the bundling of insurance, service and sometimes finance.

"The key feature is convenience — that is, the ease of having access to the 'fun parts' of a car but not having to own it," notes Henrik Littorin, marketplace director for Blocket in Sweden.

Monthly fees for subscriptions range from $300 to $500 for small- to medium-sized cars. Most subscriptions are for new vehicles. Some services take a down payment or security deposit; others aim to make subscribing as Netflix-like and simple as possible. (Carro CEO Tan goes so far as to describe his company's subscription service as "Netflix for cars.")

With most subscriptions, the customer doesn't have the option to buy the car at the end of the term. As a result, even though car subscriptions may look like shorter-term leases, they're actually closer to a rental model.

Car subscription services have been among the first players in the automotive ecosystem to fully embrace internet transactions. In general, arranging a car subscription is done entirely online — from picking out the car to finalizing payment. During the COVID-19 crisis, most car subscription companies began offering home delivery as well.

Subscription services that offer multiple brands are the norm, although some manufacturers have chosen to go it alone — Care by Volvo and Porsche Drive (formerly Porsche Passport), among others (although many OEM-sponsored programs have since shut down — more on that in a moment).

Some companies are choosing unique branding for their subscription offerings to cut some of the confusion with competing leasing or sales channels. Toyota's subscription service in Norway, for example, is perplexingly called Kinto Flex.

Who are the typical subscribers? The answer might surprise you. The average age at European subscription services including Bipi and Drover is 38.

The problem for younger customers is getting insurance at decent rates, which makes it less profitable for a car subscription service that offers one-size-fits-all pricing.

Baby boomers, on the other hand, are already comfortable with doing their own servicing and taxes; they've been doing that for decades, and don't necessarily see the advantages of a subscription.

At CarPlanner in Italy, the average driver is "45 to 55, male, professional and definitely not cash-strapped," notes CEO Marta Daina.

"People who have already arrived in their lives, rather than 18-year-olds who just got their license, see the advantages [to subscription] immediately," adds Léa Miggiano, CMO of Carvolution in Switzerland.

Subscriptions may also be a good model for new cars that aren't selling well, allowing dealers to make some residual income on those vehicles for a while, covering the initial depreciation period.

At the end of the day, though, the car in question is still a dud, and, when the subscription period is over, the company that offered the subscription (dealer, OEM or third-party marketplace) will get the car back and have to do something with it. As a result, many dealers would rather hold on to the new car, even if it's having a hard time selling, rather than "converting" it to a used vehicle.

As comedian and actor Jerry Lewis once said, "You can't polish a turd." (To which famed director Stanley Kubrick reportedly quipped, "You can if you freeze it.")

ALL'S FAIR IN LOVE AND SUBSCRIPTIONS

The highest-profile vehicle subscription service to date is — or perhaps I should say *was* — Fair, a company started by Scott Painter, the founder and former CEO of TrueCar. Painter's latest startup, Autonomy/NextCar, as I've mentioned before, is also in the subscription space — and Fair has stumbled among the potholes of an as-yet-not-fully-defined business model despite raising more than $2 billion in equity and debt.

In August 2021, Brad Stewart, the new CEO of the nearly bankrupt Fair, announced the company would be pivoting away from its subscription model and toward "an end-to-end e-commerce marketplace that offers consumers industry-best levels of inventory and comprehensive financing, insurance and extended warranties."

Stewart described the new Fair as "either Carvana without owning the cars or you can think of it as Autotrader, where you can purchase the car and have all the things that go along with it — insurance and F&I products and logistics — facilitated by that platform. In this case, us."

Before the pivot, Fair was a highflier — *the* highflier in the burgeoning subscription space — although it was spending lead investor SoftBank's cash fast and furiously. But when, in 2019, SoftBank got burned by the collapse of WeWork and the disappointing IPO of Uber, the Tokyo-based venture capital firm decided it needed to scale back the additional $500 million Fair had been hoping to raise to keep its cash-intensive business going.

SoftBank eventually came through with a bridge loan but, rather than the hundreds of millions Fair had hoped for, the total was in the tens of millions.

By November 2019, Fair had laid off nearly half its workforce of seven hundred, and Painter — along with his CFO brother, Tyler — was out. The company also halted its weekly rental program for Uber drivers and suspended downloads of its popular app.

The company turned the app back on just a few months later but limited its use to a few locations.

At its height, Fair was live in thirty-five cities across twenty-two states with four thousand dealership partners and sixty-five thousand active cars on the road. Part of the company's financing ($167 million) went to acquire Uber's XChange leasing division. XChange was rebranded as Fair Go.

Fair also acquired the car-leasing firm Canvas from Ford Credit.

Painter, meanwhile, envisions subscription sites that partner with his new company will feature the tag line, "Powered by NextCar" (or "Autonomy," as the case may be). Painter hopes to avoid Fair's fall by operating not as a consumer-facing site, but as a B2B "car-as-a-service" company.

In March 2022, Fair agreed to sell its online marketplace assets to online used vehicle retailer Shift, which will allow dealerships to list their vehicles on the online platform (similar to what Carvana has been trialing with their "Marketplace" product). Shift acquired Fair's assets for $15 million in cash and a number of shares of Class A common stock equal to 2.5% of Shift's outstanding shares. Interestingly, the purchase was funded entirely by SoftBank Group through a $20 million loan to Shift.

AUTONOMY CHANGES EVERYTHING

Enthusiasm aside, the numbers at car subscription providers are still tiny compared to the overall automotive market.

- Drover: Customers are in the low thousands.
- CarPlanner: Just over one thousand subscriptions have been sold direct to consumers in Switzerland.
- Carro: The Singapore-based company says it has "hundreds of subscribers."
- Fair.com: At its height, before the company's implosion, Fair claimed forty-five thousand subscribers in the U.S.

- Faaren: No more than twenty thousand car subscription vehicles are on the roads in Germany (not all from Faaren) compared with forty-seven *million* cars registered in the country.

"Dealers recognize that a subscription business model is coming in the longer term, and they think that it's something users will eventually want. They just don't see a big reason to push it now," explains Hilde Sommerstad, who headed Finn.no's subscription program in 2020.

Given the slow uptake, it's hard to imagine how subscriptions will grow to the 20% number McKinsey predicts by 2025.

Will electric vehicles be the catalyst? Or will real change only come with autonomous vehicles?

When fully self-driving vehicles go mainstream — whether that's in ten, twenty or thirty years — the subscription model will receive a substantial boost. While some drivers — like Monty and Emerson in our 2050 future vision — will prefer to own their autonomous vehicle, I predict that most self-driving cars will be offered according to modified ride-sharing programs.

Unlike at Uber, Lyft and Grab today, where you pay for each ride separately, autonomous vehicle subscriptions will guarantee you have access to a car when you need it without having to worry about a per-ride cost (the equivalent of a monthly transit pass, but for a private car).

A particular car may be shared between different people, or the subscription may be to whatever vehicle is closest (making it more of an autonomous taxi subscription).

DO THE ECONOMICS MAKE SENSE?

Whereas the economics for vehicle subscription services have been challenging so far, the unit economics for autonomous vehicle subscriptions are much more promising.

If Hertz owns a self-driving car that is on-the-go 24/7 (except when it has to be charged or cleaned), we can evolve from a world where vehicle capacity utilization is 4% (with the car sitting in your driveway or office parking lot for the vast majority of the day) to one where capacity utilization is near 100% and the car is constantly in circulation.

That could have the desirable benefit of driving down the costs for subscribing to a car (compared with buying it). If, before autonomy, subscriptions were slow to take off, in a self-driving world, subscriptions will become widespread.

SUBSCRIPTION CHALLENGES

Since subscriptions are very similar to rentals, the biggest concern is the same one that rental car and leasing companies face: depreciation.

As soon as the customer drives off a dealership's lot with a new car, the vehicle instantly loses a good 20% of its value. Most consumer leases are structured for three years, so the depreciation is smoothed over a longer period.

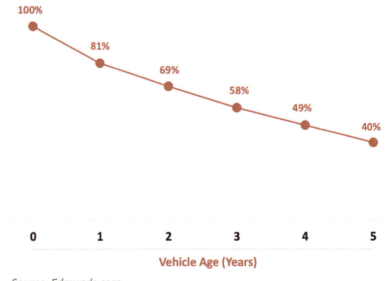

Source: Edmunds.com

For rental cars, the vehicle is "defleeted" (taken out of service) after anywhere from six months to three years, and then sold directly to a consumer or to a dealership. Vehicle depreciation is amortized over the rental or lease period, where it's built into the monthly payments and spread over the period of the rental.

For subscriptions, it's not as easy.

What happens when the vehicle is returned three months later — or less — rather than after twenty-four to thirty-six months as in today's standard leases? How do you price that kind of immediate depreciation into a subscription? Do you tack on a huge cancellation fee at the end of the lease? No one would go for that.

Reilly Brennan says that the first iteration of the subscription model has been plagued by "attracting the wrong bees to the honey. The people who wanted a subscription had poor credit and didn't know if they'd need — or be able to afford — a car in three months. They're not the Mercedes buyers."

"Subscription hasn't worked yet because there's no scale to it," Chase Fraser of FM Capital told me. "You have to own tens or even hundreds of thousands of vehicles to make the math work. Very few can do that. You've got to be someone who can keep on bankrolling the program and take massive losses."

Morgan Stanley analyst Adam Jonas believes that any future "Apple Car," especially if it's a self-driving vehicle without a steering wheel or pedals, "must be a 'shared service' and not an 'owned car.' To be clear," Jonas added, "we do not believe consumers will own title to a fully autonomous car but will engage in the service as a subscription or transport utility."

Cox Automotive has already had two forays into car subscription services — one a B2C play, which struggled and was sold; the other, a technology enabler, which is showing more staying power.

Cox established Flexdrive early in 2014 as its consumer subscription play, but it wasn't until a partnership in 2017 with Holman Enterprises that the service took off. In 2019, Flexdrive partnered with Hyundai Capital to make Hyundai vehicles available to Lyft drivers.

That turned out to be a prescient decision: In February 2020, Lyft acquired Flexdrive from Cox for $20 million plus assumption of debt and lease obligations. The Flexdrive business is now exclusive to Lyft drivers. There are fifteen thousand vehicles on the road through the program.

Cox's second subscription business has been more successful at standing on its own feet.

Cox's Clutch Technologies, as I mentioned earlier, works with more than two hundred dealers and twenty OEM brands in the U.S., Canada and Germany. Clutch focuses on luxury brands, including Porsche, BMW and Mercedes. Clutch has partnerships with AmeriDrive, which operates one of the largest subscription fleets in the U.S., and HyreCar, a marketplace for ride-sharing.

One more word about COVID-19: While it's still unclear when the pandemic will run its course, the impact on car subscriptions is already being felt.

"People saw their summer vacations canceled," explains Maximilian Renoth of Faaren. "So, they now have an extra €6,000 to spend." Renoth says that Faaren has seen an increase in luxury vehicle subscriptions. "If people can't go abroad, they'd rather subscribe to a BMW to compensate for it!"

THE LINES CAN GET BLURRY

Hertz has its fleet of cars, but it also sells vehicles direct to consumers via its retail shops and has a direct-to-dealer auction model through Hertz Dealer Direct.

So is Hertz a fleet owner, a marketplace, a dealership . . . or all three?

You could ask the same question about CarMax, which is the third largest auction company in the U.S. and the largest dealer retailer of used vehicles.

In a jaw-dropping, aggressive move, Carvana acquired ADESA's fifty-six U.S. physical auction locations for $2.2 billion, making it both the second largest used vehicle retailer, as well as the second largest auction company in the U.S.

To further complicate matters, Hertz is piloting a new subscription program called MyCar in Austin, Atlanta and Southwest Florida. The cost is more than the typical subscription services — from $999 to $1,399 a month — although Hertz allows you to swap cars twice a month.

European rental giant Sixt has a somewhat more affordable program; a Kia Rio runs $459 a month, plus $199 to sign up. A BMW X1 starts at $899 a month.

In the U.S., the Sixt+ subscription service is currently available in Washington, California, Nevada, Texas, Florida and Georgia.

Hyundai has announced a hybrid subscription-purchase option. In order to promote its new electric Ioniq 5 crossover, the automaker plans to offer shoppers a few months behind the wheel as a subscription before their final decision. The subscription will cover the vehicle, insurance and maintenance.

OEM SUBSCRIPTION FAILS

The automotive news site Jalopnik reports that there were once nineteen car subscription services in the U.S., nine of them offered by OEMs. Yet, as of mid-2021, nearly all have dropped or substantially scaled back their nascent subscription programs, including once high-profile manufacturers such as BMW, Genesis, Mercedes-Benz, Nissan and Audi.

- Cadillac and BMW have both said they're reevaluating and retooling their programs, so they may not be gone forever.
- Jaguar Land Rover's subscription service, Pivotal, is still operating — but in the U.K. only.
- Genesis's Spectrum program can be found at several dealerships in Florida . . . and in South Korea.
- Ford's Canvas subscription service, launched in 2017, lasted just two years before lack of demand left it sputtering, ultimately to be acquired by Fair.

Mid-decade, the assumption was that "we'd all be transitioning in a driverless car utopia, and single-person car ownership would be a thing of the past," writes Jalopnik's Lawrence Hodge. "People would simply order up an autonomous vehicle from a free-roaming fleet to get to their destinations. Since no one would actually buy cars, people would subscribe to use them, essentially ending car ownership as we currently know it."

The problem was, the industry believed that autonomous vehicles would be coming sooner than they are.

Another problem: Subscriptions are perceived as more expensive than leasing.

"A lessee looking at an Escalade at the time Book by Cadillac [the OEM's nascent subscription service] was operational would have found that, even at a maximum of forty-eight months and 15,000 miles, one would come out over $700 cheaper leasing than subscribing," Hodge notes, while adding that this, of course, "isn't factoring in the substantial down payment required with most leases. [Still], you have to wonder if most people who could afford one of these services would simply prefer to own or lease a car."

WHO CAN BEST CAPITALIZE ON SUBSCRIPTIONS?

The final question I want to raise may be the most important to readers of this book: Who will be best positioned to offer subscriptions — the OEMs, the dealers or the fleets?

The answer, as I see it today (and anything can change), is the OEMs, although they clearly have more to learn to drive consumer adoption.

Questions that still need to be addressed by the OEMs include:

- 🚗 Who will handle the vehicle service when the subscription comes from the manufacturer? Will consumers be allowed to choose their franchise dealer, or will it be dictated to them?
- 🚗 Who manages service if subscription is via a fleet provider? Will franchise dealers get any of this business?

- Can the OEMs make the service affordable? Of all the OEM-backed subscription programs I've seen, Porsche Drive is by far the most expensive — $1,500 to $2,600 per month for a single vehicle and from $2,100 to $3,100 per month for a multi-vehicle subscription plan, which allows you to swap cars at will. Porsche's service, like most, is limited by location, offered in only nine U.S. cities for now, including Atlanta, Las Vegas and Los Angeles.

VOLVO AS A MODEL?

Given the challenges faced by OEMs, then, perhaps the most likely future scenario will be hybrid. Let's take another look at Care by Volvo's subscription program, which I discussed in the previous chapter.

Care by Volvo offers drivers an "all-inclusive" two-year subscription service including maintenance, insurance, tire and wheel protection, all for a flat monthly fee. In the U.K., there are two options: a three-year term with no deposit or sign-up fee, and Care by Volvo Flexible, which offers an open-ended three-month rolling contract after an initial risk-free thirty-day trial period.

The program had to be redesigned, you'll recall, after the California New Car Dealers Association filed a petition with the state's New Motor Vehicle Board contending that Volvo was undermining "the traditional role of Volvo dealer franchisees."

Version 2.0 "was created in partnership with Volvo retailers and further expands consumer choice by allowing them to select a vehicle from retailer inventory," the company said in a statement.

The Care by Volvo website instructs users to "subscribe [then] choose your preferred retailer, and we will contact you to schedule a time to pick up your vehicle." Pickup is "within two weeks of order confirmation." You can cancel your subscription after five months (except in Illinois, which requires a full year's commitment). Costs range from $600 to $750 a month, not including tax.

Care by Volvo now accounts for 6% of the brand's new-vehicle sales in the United States and more than 10% in Europe, well beyond the 5% total targeted for the service in its first year. In the U.K., that's equal to 2,500 cars delivered or 15% of Volvo's retail sales in the country. Of those, 33% of subscriptions were for the brand's Volvo Recharge plug-in hybrids.

Even more impressive, Volvo reports that 91% of its subscription customers are new to the Volvo brand.

I have no doubt that subscriptions are coming in some form. While autonomy may be the catalyst that really drives adoption, the OEMs will continue to tinker in the short term to work on business models that offer more flexibility and convenience to consumers while helping them to differentiate and sell more vehicles.

CHAPTER SIX

AUTONOMY

"People are so bad at driving cars that computers don't have to be that good to be much better."
— Marc Andreessen, partner at Andreessen Horowitz

Intel's $15.3 billion acquisition of Jerusalem-based Mobileye in 2017 surprised many automotive industry observers. After all, what did the world's leading semiconductor maker need with a software and hardware system that alerts drivers when they're getting too close to the car in front of them or veering out of their lane?

But Mobileye had been working on much more than lane-control software; the company has developed a complete solution for self-driving cars and Intel was eager to play catch up in order not to cede to Apple, Waymo and Tesla what may prove to be the most revolutionary change to driving in one hundred years.

The fruits of the Mobileye acquisition became apparent in 2021, when Intel announced that it would be launching the world's first commercial robo-taxi service in two locations: Tel Aviv and Munich.

The pilot, due to start in 2022, will include eight six-seater compact electric SUVs from Chinese manufacturer NIO, decked out with Mobileye's "Drive" autonomous vehicle system. Mobileye will own the fleet of cars while European rental company Sixt will operate and maintain them. Mobileye is also in talks with German car manufacturers about expanding its platform for self-driving cars to additional OEMs.

The NIO SE8 has a range of around 300 miles and will offer Level 4 automation, which provides for a self-driving experience without a human behind the wheel, in a limited area (although there will still be a person in each vehicle who can manually override the system when necessary).

The self-driving NIOs will have eleven sensors around the car — at the front, at the rear, inside the body, on the side mirrors and on top of the vehicle. These include both longer-range lidar ("light detection and ranging") and radar ("radio detection and ranging").

"This will be the most beautiful self-driving robo-taxi in the world," Johann Jungwirth, Mobileye's vice president of mobility-as-a-service, told the *Jerusalem Post*. "We designed the cameras in the roof unit in a way that makes the technology almost invisible, unlike other robo-taxi models being used."

Mobileye is starting with taxis rather than private cars due to the high costs of outfitting existing vehicles with an autonomous driving "kit," which can run as high as $20,000 per car. Mobileye co-founder and CEO Amnon Shashua estimates that the price will drop to just $5,000 by the middle of the decade as Intel-developed lidar and radar components come online.

Taxis also make sense because the main cost is not the vehicle as much as the driver.

"If you remove the driver from the equation, you get a return on an investment," Shashua notes.

One more advantage: A taxi can travel on a set route — even in a bus lane — rather than needing the ability to go anywhere, as with a private car. That simplifies operation and improves safety — at least during the test period.

Users of the Intel/Mobileye pilot will hail a self-driving taxi using either an app from Moovit, the Israel-based public transportation mapping company Intel acquired in 2020 for just under $1 billion, or Sixt's own ONE app. The taxis will sport both Moovit and Sixt branding so they can be easily distinguished by potential riders.

Of all the changes coming to automotive retailing, self-driving vehicles have the potential to be the most disruptive. And yet the timeline remains elusive, at least for consumer (as opposed to commercial) use cases.

What was originally supposed to be just around the corner is now looking increasingly remote; the 2050 date mentioned in my opening chapter might not be so far-fetched. Intel/Mobileye's pilot seems tantalizingly close, but full Level 5 autonomy, not just on controlled, fixed routes, is proving to be technically challenging. Apple is hinting at an accelerated rollout for its autonomous project, but it's all rumors for now.

In this chapter, I will try to address the following questions:

- Why is it taking so long to get to full autonomy? When will autonomy move beyond the semifunctional "autopilot" features that are currently being promoted as autonomous driving (even though they're anything but that)?
- Who will be first to offer a commercial system at scale? Tesla? Apple? Intel? Alphabet's Waymo?
- What potential pitfalls — safety, regulations, technical mishaps — may derail our autonomous future?
- Will autonomous vehicles prove to be safer? Will human drivers ultimately be banned?
- How will autonomy affect how dealers do business?

LEVELS OF AUTONOMY

The autonomous industry has defined six levels of autonomy:

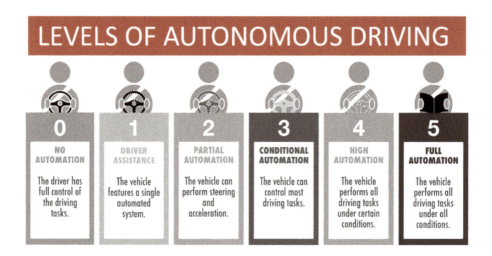

LEVEL 0 – NO DRIVING AUTOMATION

A human driver is completely responsible for controlling the vehicle, although there can be a variety of safety features, such as backup cameras, collision and blind-spot warnings, emergency braking and lane-keeping assistance. These are considered Level 0 because they don't drive the vehicle but only offer alerts or momentary actions in specific situations. Virtually all cars on the roads today are Level 0.

LEVEL 1 – DRIVER ASSISTANCE

This is where there is at least one driver-support system involving braking, steering or acceleration. Adaptive cruise control is an example of Level 1 automation. It maintains a safe distance between your vehicle and the traffic ahead without any human intervention required, but the car still requires an active driver.

LEVEL 2 – PARTIAL AUTOMATION OR ADAS (ADVANCED DRIVER ASSISTANCE SYSTEMS)

The vehicle can take over steering, acceleration and braking, but the driver must remain at the wheel, alert and ready to jump into action. Tesla's Autopilot; Ford's BlueCruise; Highway Driving Assist installed in Genesis, Hyundai and Kia vehicles; Toyota's Advanced Drive; Lexus Teammate; and GM's Cruise systems (formerly branded as Cruise Automation) are all examples of Level 2 automation.

LEVEL 3 – CONDITIONAL DRIVING AUTOMATION

You're stuck in a traffic jam, and there you are, reading a newspaper. That's the promise of Level 3, where drivers don't have to actively steer or brake in specific situations but cannot doze off, as they must be ready to take over if the situation changes. Vehicles must monitor the driver's state (through cameras) to make sure he or she is ready to snap back when required and has not fallen asleep at the wheel. Audi was the first to develop a Level 3 product (its "traffic jam assistance" technology), although it never received regulatory approval. Honda is now working on its own version, as is Mercedes-Benz. "The drivers are still there" in Level 3, Shashua notes. "They are still responsible, but the burden of driving is reduced — and the chance of an accident is also reduced, because the systems are very safe." Level 2 ADAS and Level 3 conditional driving automation can "get us to 80% of the safety of a full autonomous vehicle for much less cost," industry expert Glenn Mercer told me, citing data from automotive technology supplier Aptiv.

LEVEL 4 – HIGH DRIVING AUTOMATION

Finally, you can take a nap! Level 4 autonomy does not require any human interaction in the vehicle's operation. Such a vehicle may not even have a steering wheel or pedal. Level 4 may not work if there is severe weather or limited visibility, in which case the vehicle will alert the driver and shut off until the bad weather passes. Level 4 vehicles are currently limited to certain geographies and slow speeds (30 miles per hour in an urban environment). Waymo's autonomous tests in Arizona have been Level 4.

LEVEL 5 – FULL DRIVING AUTOMATION

Now we're cooking with gas (or lithium-ion batteries, since most autonomous vehicles will be electric). These cars can go anywhere and do anything an experienced human driver can do. Level 5 vehicles won't have steering wheels, brakes or pedals, and may have "smart cabins" designed very differently than passenger cars today.

Morgan Stanley predicts 2% of all cars sold in 2030 will have Level 5 autonomy, comprising 0.5% of global miles traveled. By 2040, that number jumps to 7.6% and by 2050 it climbs to 47% of miles traveled.

"If our goal is to eliminate over 90% of crashes, we really need to go for Level 4 and Level 5, full autonomous," says Shashua.

"I believe the right thing to do is to get the driver out of the loop altogether," adds Larry Burns, GM's former corporate vice president for research, development and planning. "The situational awareness challenge of asking someone to reengage in the driving task when they've been sitting there not driving for twenty or thirty minutes is a tougher problem to solve than getting the system to autonomously handle 99.99% of the stuff that happens in the world. I believe the objective should be to get to Level 4, starting in a geo-fenced area that's big enough to have commercial value."

Level 4 does have some usage limitations. "For example, it doesn't travel in the rain," Shashua notes. "In the fifth stage, there will be no usage limitations. Driving will be possible in any situation and in every place."

Mobileye's approach to autonomy, like most of its competitors, starts by building a detailed three-dimensional map. This painstaking process must be done again and again, city by city.

First, ordinary cars are equipped with lidar sensors that measure distances using pulses of light. Company workers drive test cars around the city to collect the data needed to generate the map, including measuring the distance to every curb, median and roadside tree.

The autonomous vehicles use lidar to monitor their surroundings, comparing what they "see" with what's on the map and alerting the vehicle to any worrisome nearby objects (other cars, pedestrians, bicycles). The radar and other cameras enhance the sensing capabilities.

Tesla is taking a very different approach.

The company has argued that autonomous vehicles can understand their surroundings merely by capturing what a human driver would see. That means the cars need only one kind of sensor — cameras — and since Tesla's cars are already equipped with cameras, the company argues it can transform them into autonomous vehicles by gradually improving the vehicle's existing software.

It's not clear yet who will win this battle. There may be space for both approaches.

Burns admits that he was nervous the first time he stepped into a fully autonomous vehicle.

"My hands were shaking over the steering wheel," he reports. "My feet were nervous over the pedals. But within five minutes, I was relaxed; I realized this car was doing everything I would do as a driver and even better. I think this is all about people understanding what's possible in their lives and what's possible with the technology. I worry about people coming to a premature judgment and therefore resisting."

DealerScience founder Andrew Gordon likens the push toward a fully autonomous future to "herd immunity for AVs." Once we have enough Level 3 and Level 4 cars out there, it makes Level 5 safer for everyone, he told me.

ACCIDENTS WILL HAPPEN

One of the key advantages of autonomous vehicles is that they are safer than those piloted by human drivers. Mobileye's Shashua says an autonomous vehicle has only one-thousandth the likelihood of being in an accident compared with one driven by a person.

In the U.S., an individual has a statistical average of one collision for every 500,000 miles of travel and a risk of one death for every 94 million miles driven. (Worldwide, it's one death for every 60 million miles driven.) Some 1.5 million people are killed in traffic accidents worldwide each year.

Self-driving cars will allow accidents to "reach a stage of close to zero," Shashua says. "This is very good news for society and for the economy."

But it's going to be a tough sell to legislators (and to pedestrians) who remember highly publicized autonomous driving fails.

The most infamous so far was when a self-driving car killed Elaine Herzberg in the outskirts of Tempe, Arizona, in 2018.

In that incident, Uber was running an autonomous test of a Volvo SUV with a backup driver behind the wheel. The vehicle, traveling at around 40 miles per hour, apparently couldn't recognize that pedestrians sometimes jaywalk, which is what Herzberg was doing at 10 p.m. as she wheeled her bicycle across a mostly deserted street in the city's outskirts.

Uber's autonomous software at that time was able to identify pedestrians in crosswalks but not in other situations, according to a report by the National Transportation Safety Board. The software only realized there was a problem too late and concluded it needed to brake just 1.3 seconds before the fatal collision.

Uber says it "has since modified its programming to include jaywalkers among its recognized objects."

To make matters worse, the backup driver in the Tempe crash, Rafaela Vasquez, was not doing her job, but instead was watching a streaming episode of *The Voice* on her mobile phone, according to records from video service Hulu.

User error is a common denominator behind many of the accidents that have occurred in recent years with self-driving vehicles. To be sure, the cars are making errors, but the backup drivers have not been paragons of responsibility.

That's what happened in 2021 when two men in Texas were killed in their 2019 Tesla Model S. Minutes before the crash, the men were talking about the vehicle's so-called Autopilot feature. Autopilot is, as noted above, Level 1 autonomy; it should never be left to its own driving devices.

Autopilot was also the cause of a 2016 crash in Florida, also in a Tesla Model S, where the vehicle failed to brake for a tractor-trailer that made a left turn in front of it.

Days before the tragedy that killed Herzberg, Robbie Miller, a Tesla operations manager, alerted company executives that its self-driving cars were "routinely in accidents," partly due to faults with the technology but also because of the "poor behavior" of operators.

"A car was damaged nearly every other day in February 2018," Miller noted. "We shouldn't be hitting things every 15,000 miles!"

Some have bemoaned the eagerness with which autonomous tests are being rolled out.

Jason Levine, former executive director of the Center for Auto Safety, expressed concern that the National Highway Traffic Safety Administration is too focused on "enabling the rapid deployment of self-driving vehicles by amending rules written for cars with drivers. [That] may be the fastest way to authorize the deployment of autonomous vehicles, but it is not a consumer safety-driven approach."

That's backed up by an alarming counterpoint to Shashua's optimistic safety scenario: According to research conducted by the University of Michigan, the number of accidents in self-driving cars is 9.1 per million miles driven, compared with only 4.1 crashes per million miles driven in conventional vehicles.

It's still quite low — suggesting that concerns over autonomous safety may be blown out of proportion — but at least for the present moment, it's still more than twice the rate of human-driven cars.

The good news: Crashes in AVs were generally less serious, taking place at lower speeds. And the gloomy numbers might not be entirely fair, as human drivers tend not to report minor accidents.

What accident rate would be acceptable? Do self-driving cars need to be 10% safer? 100%?

Here's what consumers are saying about their comfort level in regard to riding in an autonomous vehicle, according to various surveys:

CONSUMER CONFIDENCE RIDING IN AUTONOMOUS VEHICLES

16% would feel comfortable riding in a self-driving car.

61% are not ready to ride in a self-driving car.

75% would rather drive their own car than ride in an autonomous vehicle.

76% want Congress to mandate brakes in self-driving cars.

68% would need a self-driving vehicle to be at least 5x safer than a human-driven one.

57% would need to understand who is legally responsible in the event of a crash.

WHO'S TO BLAME?

That question — and its answer — is still evolving, with the blame (or cause) of the accident murky at best.

"Let's say I want to move into a different lane in heavy traffic," explains Shashua, referring to human-driven vehicles. "If I just signal, no one will let me make the move. I need to get the driver behind me in the lane next to me to slow down, so I start signaling. I signal and start to squeeze in, and at some stage, he'll get the hint and let me in. If he doesn't get the hint, I'll give up. I'll let him pass me and try to squeeze in again — until in the end, I'll manage to switch lanes."

But what happens if another driver runs into your self-driving car while it's trying to change lanes? Who's to blame in that case?

"I'll claim that they were dreaming and didn't notice that I wanted to enter their lane; they'll claim I was reckless. In the end, a court will make a decision. But that's not consistent with the way we want to design a robot," Shashua continues, the robot being the car's self-driving smarts. "So, what do I tell the robot to do — 'Wait until the driver in the other lane makes room for you to squeeze in'? We need to create a transparent model [so] the public will know [exactly] what the robot does."

In the case of the crash that killed Elaine Herzberg, the driver was charged with negligent homicide. Uber was not charged (Herzberg's family settled with Uber out of court), and Vasquez pleaded not guilty.

"As long as self-driving cars still need a human safety driver behind the wheel, there will be confusion about whose fault it is when something goes wrong," the BBC points out.

Burns acknowledges the risks but is adamant that the benefits of self-driving cars outweigh the concerns.

"This is a once-in-a-century opportunity to simultaneously deal with 1.3 million fatalities worldwide per year on roadways," he says, "as well as to deal with congestion, to deal with dependence on oil in transportation, to deal with the land use that comes with three parking spots per car in the United States, and to deal with equality of access. The deaths and injuries from crashes alone — it's epidemic in scale."

One way of mitigating consumer concerns is to limit where an autonomous vehicle can drive — at least, at first.

Imagine a city that's built on a grid, as most U.S. cities are. What if we designated every other street only for autonomous vehicles? The streets would essentially act like horizontal elevator shafts: They go back and forth in a straight line. They don't go around curves.

In a "street elevator" like this, self-driving cars could operate with significantly reduced concern of accidents. That works best for autonomous transit vehicles and robo-taxis.

The elevator metaphor is even more relevant when you recall that elevator cabins used to have operators. Now they operate independently. They're already self-driving vehicles.

Repairify's Tony Rimas agrees that the first widescale deployment of autonomous vehicles may be in dedicated lanes but questions the usefulness.

"If that's the case, why don't I just take the high-speed rail?" he asks.

Rimas also wonders whether the technical complexity of vehicle autonomy will result in insurers being quicker to declare a total loss in case of an accident, because the cars are too expensive to repair.

Burns remains upbeat and likens the move to self-driving cars to eradicating disease.

"If I had just created a cure for cancer and it held promise to save a lot of people with cancer, but some could still die from the treatment, I think we'd get on with it; we'd find a way to manage that. We ought to look at autonomous vehicles as a cure for the roadway transportation epidemic and think about their deployment the way we test and deploy vaccines."

CYBERATTACKS

Another potential pitfall for autonomous vehicles — and one that may loom larger in consumers' concerns as it becomes more common — is hackers taking control of a car and causing an accident by disabling the brakes or steering the vehicle off the road.

It's not an idle threat.

In 2015, hackers remotely took over a Jeep, forcing it to stop on a St. Louis highway while driving at 80 miles per hour. The hackers were able to access the car's braking and steering through the onboard entertainment system, a well-known vulnerability.

The 2015 hack remains relatively isolated and it's not clear that vehicle hacks are going to catch on for one main reason: money.

"There are many reasons we see cyberattacks — some for money, some for terror and some just because a hacker can do it," says Chuck Brokish, director of automotive business development at Green Hills Software, which builds programming tools for embedded systems.

"Most of the time, there needs to be a financial incentive to spend the resources to perform such attacks."

"There isn't really that much money to be made in taking control of a vehicle on the road," adds Chris Urmson, founder and CEO of Aurora, which provides transportation software for the trucking industry.

If there is, in fact, money to be made, it may come in the form of ransomware.

As cars begin to log more and more of their users' activities — travel habits, location of the vehicle and more — and if cars begin to include their own digital wallets to make online purchases, that data could become valuable to a hacker and could prompt a panicked driver to pay the ransom. Data from a driver's mobile device, if it's paired with the car's entertainment and GPS system, could give an added incentive to an unscrupulous hacker.

"Cars increasingly contain a treasure trove of personal information that could be valuable to hackers, from location and biometric data to passwords for connected devices," observes Rebecca Baden Chaney, a partner in Crowell & Moring's mass tort, transportation and digital transformation practices. "And unlike laptops and cell phones, for which users are more familiar with how to protect themselves, vehicle owners may not be as proactive in protecting data in their vehicles."

Automotive Ventures has invested in Privacy4Cars, a startup that helps wipe personal data that may have been synchronized from a consumer's phone. The company estimates that four out of every five cars sold in the last year contain some personal information.

"If you bring back your lease, trade-in or rental, and that information is not deleted, it's going to stay in there forever," Privacy4Cars CEO Andrea Amico told ABC7 TV in Chicago. "The apps you're using, emails, logins to different services, not to mention metadata associated with your phone . . . makes it easy to reidentify you. If you have a vehicle with GPS, it will have all your breadcrumbs: where you've been, where you live, maybe your garage door codes. If you have medical info, you may be in violation of HIPAA, the Health Insurance Portability and Accountability Act of 1996."

A hacker could "brick" a self-driving vehicle until a ransom is paid, or the car could be reprogrammed to drive to the hacker's location.

Perhaps the biggest concern: If hackers could gain access to a fleet of vehicles, they could, in theory, require a ransom from the fleet owner to regain access to its cars.

"There is no longer much of a difference between hacking a computer and hacking a connected vehicle," explains Steve Wernikoff, a litigation partner at Detroit-headquartered law firm Honigman LLP, who previously served as a senior enforcement attorney at the Federal Trade Commission. "A connected vehicle is a computer, or rather a set of computers." And while most of these hacks are theoretical at this point and have only been proven possible in extremely controlled research scenarios, "in light of the potential profit and harm that can be done by such hacks, the motivation to attempt them likely will continue."

WHO ARE THE PLAYERS?

TechCrunch reports that there are today around 1,400 autonomous vehicles on public roads in the U.S., from about eighty different companies. Some sixty-two of those companies are registered in California alone.

The leaders, as I've listed earlier, are companies such as Waymo, Apple, Intel/Mobileye, GM's Cruise and Tesla. These are the players I'd watch carefully.

That said, most OEMs have their own self-driving programs as well, including Audi/Volkswagen, BMW, Daimler and Mercedes-Benz.

Ford CEO Mark Fields predicted in 2015 that fully autonomous vehicles would be on U.S. streets within four years. While in hindsight we can see that Fields was a tad too ambitious in his prognosis, Ford remains hard at work developing its self-driving strategy with Argo AI and partner Lyft; the latter is looking to build out its robo-taxi business.

Third-party vendors building their own cars or providing some of the hardware or software required to power the autonomous future include:

- Cruise — which has partnerships with Honda and GM and is majority-owned by GM.
- Zoox — acquired in 2020 by Amazon, Zoox is launching a trial of its self-driving software in rainy Seattle to "see how water impacts the sensors," the company's CTO Jesse Levinson says.
- Chinese autonomous startups AutoX and DeepRoute.ai — both have received investments from Alibaba.
- Teague — which is partnering with other AV companies to build, among other projects, a self-driving yellow school bus.
- Aurora, Innoviz, Luminar, Nauto, Optimus Ride, Pony.ai and Transdev.

Venture capitalist Chase Fraser suggests that the smart money is on the tech giants. He's betting on Google most of all.

"They will get so deep into the car business. They will pull off a sexy version of this. They have the cash that others don't, which they can use to buy massive fleets," Fraser told me.

The media has contributed to the hype.

"When we started hearing about autonomous vehicles a few years ago in a big way, VCs started chasing Level 4 and Level 5 autonomy plays. But they were not ready. And they're still not ready," Fraser notes.

Fraser's firm is not investing in those high-end deals, he says. "From a VC standpoint, we need to make money in the next seven to eight years." Autonomy is not near-enough term "where we as a fund can get involved."

Volkswagen CEO Herbert Diess clearly wants his firm to play a leading role in the autonomous future. At the 2021 IAA Mobility car show in Munich, Diess commented that autonomous vehicles and software, rather than electric cars and batteries, are "going to change our industry like nothing else before."

Volkswagen has put money behind its intentions to become a leading autonomous player: In 2020, the company invested $2.6 billion in Pittsburgh-based self-driving car startup Argo AI, integrating VW's own self-driving subsidiary, AID (Autonomous Intelligent Driving), into Argo AI and expanding Argo's workforce to more than one thousand in the U.S. and Europe.

Argo AI had already received a $1 billion investment from Ford in 2017. Ford and VW are sharing the costs of further developing Argo's software. Ford announced in 2018 that it would spend $4 billion through 2023 to build out its autonomous vehicle business, creating a new subsidiary, Ford Autonomous Vehicles.

At the IAA event in Germany, VW and Argo demonstrated a self-driving all-electric micro-bus dubbed the ID. Buzz AD (for autonomous driving). Like Mobileye's robo-taxi tests, the ID. Buzz will first hit the streets of Munich with the aim of deploying a full commercial service in Hamburg by 2025. That will be through VW's mobility-as-a-service division, MOIA. The van sports six lidar, eleven radar and fourteen cameras distributed over the vehicle.

Earlier in 2021, Ford and Argo announced plans to deploy one thousand self-driving vehicles on Lyft's ride-hailing network over the next five years, starting in Miami and Austin.

Self-driving shuttles between airport terminals and rental-car facilities, or between the parking lot and a sports stadium, could also come sooner rather than later. They're slow-moving, so there's less chance for injury.

GM's majority-owned Cruise self-driving car subsidiary plans to launch a fleet of robo-taxis in Dubai beginning in 2023, using purpose-built Cruise Origin vehicles. Dubai will be the first city outside the U.S. where Cruise will operate. (San Francisco will be the test city in the U.S.)

By 2030, Cruise and Dubai's transit authority hope to have four thousand robo-taxis in operation. Cruise will be the exclusive service provider in the Emirates until 2029.

None of those primarily robo-taxi and ride-hailing plays are going to make a huge impact on dealerships that serve consumers, but it's an indication of where the industry is going and a proof of concept for autonomy in general.

"People ask me a lot, 'Who's going to win?'" muses Burns. "I think you're going to see an ecosystem emerge not unlike the one that emerged with the internet. I'm not at all convinced that there's going to be a single vertically integrated player that emerges from this that can do the driving system, the vehicle, the transportation system operations, the brand building and all of that. I think you're going to see quite a bit of codependency emerge."

Burns adds that the company that comes out on top will not be whoever has the coolest "chrome and fenders and fascia. It's going to be very much the overall experience that customers have, and that experience is going to be determined more by software and data and analytics than the traditional basis of competition in the auto industry."

WHITHER APPLE?

Apple has long been rumored to be working on a next-generation car. At first, Apple's plans were dismissed as most likely just an enhanced version of the company's CarPlay software. Then the rumors shifted to an electric battery-powered car.

Finally, in late 2021, *Bloomberg* broke the story that Apple had made a strategic decision to shift the focus of its "Project Titan" to produce a fully self-driving car, not just a more conventional vehicle with semi-autonomous features.

New project leader Kevin Lynch said he wanted the very first Apple Car to drive itself, *Bloomberg* reported. The launch — expected by 2025 — is significantly more aggressive than Apple's original rumored timeline that pegged 2028 as self-driving showtime.

The Apple autonomous vehicle is said to have lounge-like seating for passengers, an infotainment system resembling a large iPad, and no steering wheel or pedals (so it's Level 5 from the get-go). Apple initially held talks with Canoo in 2020 to design the vehicle's interior, but ultimately chose not to move forward.

The Apple Car will be powered in part by an Apple-designed chip strong enough to handle the AI requirements of self-driving cars. TSMC, the same company that makes chips for the iPhone, iPad and Mac, is expected to manufacture the chip.

The only official announcement Apple has made about its self-driving car plans came from CEO Tim Cook in 2017.

"We're focusing on autonomous systems," he said. "It's a core technology that we view as very important. We sort of see it as the mother of all AI projects. It's probably one of the most difficult AI projects actually to work on."

Apple has no experience making cars, so the company is expected to partner with an existing auto manufacturer. The name bandied about the most has been Hyundai. There was apparently discussion on transferring the Apple Car development and manufacturing to Hyundai's Kia brand and assembly lines in the U.S., but that didn't pan out.

The deal with Hyundai, if it were to happen, is rumored to be worth nearly $4 billion, although Hyundai said in February 2021 that it is not in discussions with Apple. (South Korean media strongly suggested that the partnership may yet survive.)

Hyundai's concerns appear to be centered around how an Apple-branded car would hurt Hyundai's own vehicle sales. Apple is said to be considering working with Foxconn on the Apple autonomous vehicle; Foxconn already makes most of Apple's iPhones and is not a car-making competitor. Canada-based mobility tech company Magna has been suggested as another option, as is the possibility Apple may try to manufacture the vehicle itself.

If Apple does jump into the game, it will have to innovate its way to the top. If the rumors are correct, the first version of an Apple Car could have a range of over 300 miles on a full charge and could be charged up to 80% in just eighteen minutes.

BEYOND THE PASSENGER CAR – THE COMMERCIAL USE CASE

Phantom Auto is not a self-driving car company per se but provides human-assisted remote backup driving in case a car — or its driver — gets stuck (especially important when there isn't a physical steering wheel in the car).

In an interesting pivot, Phantom realized that the consumer self-driving market has been slower to take off than expected and, as a result, is — for now — focusing on emergency remote control for forklifts and "yard trucks."

That makes sense, says Reilly Brennan of Trucks VC (which is not, as its name suggests, solely focused on commercial vehicles). "Autonomous vehicles are quite viable even today in off-road environments. Not on public roads with passengers, where you need to get from point A to point B in a certain time. I call it 'structured autonomy,' where it performs a specific task in a specific environment over and over."

While autonomy may remain an edge case for consumers for the next decade, it will become very common for tasks such as shuttling goods, and not human cargo.

Self-driving trucks may be among the first out of the gate; that's in large part because the economic argument is crystal clear: An autonomous truck could drive nonstop from Los Angeles to Orlando at 100 miles an hour. No need for a break or to switch drivers midway. And trucks mostly stick to the highways where dedicated truck lanes could be set up (and in many cases, already exist).

Tesla is working on a self-driving truck, as is Isuzu, which will install technology from autonomous vehicle vendor Gatik on its medium-size N-Series models.

The Gatik system is supposed to create a Level 4 self-driving vehicle; the first pilots were due to launch by the end of 2021. A test electric-powered autonomous vehicle at a Walmart in Louisiana is already underway.

A Gatik-powered self-driving vehicle moves items along a 2-mile route from a Walmart "dark store" (one that stocks items for fulfillment but isn't open to the public) to a nearby Walmart neighborhood store.

Gatik has a similar multiyear partnership with Canadian grocery chain Loblaws.

FedEx announced in September 2021 it would begin testing self-driving trucks on the 500-mile round-trip route between Dallas and Houston. The pilot is based on autonomous driving software from Aurora and PACCAR's vehicle platform. FedEx said the trucks will complete the route several times a week. While they will be running autonomously, the trucks will have a backup driver for safety.

Other models in the delivery truck and van space include Ford's E-Transit Cargo Van, Bollinger's Deliver-E-van and GM's BrightDrop delivery van. These are currently just electric vehicles rather than self-driving ones, although Rivian's Driver+, a semi-autonomous driving technology, is similar to Tesla's Autopilot.

Autonomous trucking firm Embark takes a different approach to autonomous trucking: As opposed to manufacturing and operating a fleet of trucks, Embark offers its autonomous software as a service. Carriers and fleets will pay a per-mile subscription fee and will purchase trucks with compatible hardware directly from OEMs. The company recently went public on the Nasdaq exchange at a $5 billion valuation.

Bringing deliveries closer to home — quite literally — self-driving startup Nuro announced in 2021 a partnership with Domino's in Houston to bring fresh, hot pizza to consumers' residences. The California-based startup previously partnered with CVS, Walgreens and Kroger.

Nuro's second-generation vehicle, the R2, is the first self-driving car that's legally allowed to operate without side mirrors or a windshield. It has a speed limit of 25 miles an hour.

Customers can track their Nuro's location, and, when the order arrives at the curbside destination, the user will receive a security code to open the cargo compartment.

WHO WILL OWN AUTONOMOUS VEHICLES?

I posed this question in the previous chapter regarding subscriptions, but it bears repeating because it will have such a large potential impact on dealerships.

Burns has a good way of analyzing the parameters.

"There are almost two hundred million cars and trucks in the United States and a lot of people who want to have their own," he said in an interview with the car website *Jalopnik*. In the U.S. — and in China, too — cars are a status symbol and a rite of passage. "So, I've given thought to the idea of an autonomous vehicle that can be for personal use as well as shared use, because I think the future is going to be both of those."

How might that work?

"If you have an autonomous vehicle for your own personal use, you'll likely want to be picked up at your door and dropped off at your

CHAPTER SIX   123

door. And you won't want to be hassled with parking your vehicle; you'll want that vehicle to be smart enough to go somewhere and refuel or recharge and wait for you. I think that vehicle would get a lot more usage than my personal car now. When I arrive at work, it drops me off at the door, and then I could dispatch it in the middle of the day to go pick up my dry cleaning, and I could dispatch it again to go get takeout dinner and then go pick up my kids and then pick me up at work and take me back home. This whole world of a robotic personal valet is very intriguing to me; I think it's going to eliminate the need for owning a second and third car initially and, ultimately, owning a car altogether."

One other benefit that Burns didn't mention: A self-driving car could drive itself to a dealer or repair facility for routine maintenance. If dealers were to switch to a 24/7 model, we could see most repairs taking place at night, so that owners wouldn't be inconvenienced during regular work hours. Ditto for autonomous vehicles driving themselves to a charge spot. (The charging nozzles will have to be replaced by something more wireless.)

What will all those autonomous vehicles plying our city streets do for congestion and traffic jams?

Some say it will make traffic worse, leading to more single passengers in a car at the expense of ride-share vehicles or public transportation.

Shashua says numbers he's crunched show a different picture.

One calculation focused on San Francisco, where there are sixty thousand Uber and Lyft vehicles transporting people.

"It turned out that the same number of passengers could be transported with two thousand autonomous vehicles," Shashua points out.

Burns ran simulations of his own, asking the question, "To make all the one- or two-person trips that automobiles currently make, how many tailor-designed driverless electric vehicles would you need? In city after city that we studied, you could replace all of the cars with a fleet that's 15% the size. In simulations, those vehicles were picking people up in two to three minutes. A properly managed, optimized fleet would take a lot of cars out of the system."

"To make them profitable, many industry experts estimate that autonomous vehicles would need to operate fifteen to twenty hours a day," adds Dennis Clark, formerly at Honda.

There's also a societal benefit.

"Some worry that additional road miles from both shared and personal usage will cause more congestion, but for those people who are taking trips they couldn't before — due to their age or a disability, for example — and are now able to participate more in society and the economy, that's a good thing," Burns says. "We should be celebrating those miles!"

I sometimes like to think of autonomous vehicles as being in a polyamorous relationship: The car may be promiscuous, but it always comes home by morning and, in some cases, will be your most loyal companion.

WHAT ABOUT THE COSTS?

How would shared autonomous vehicles be priced?

- It could be a flat recurring fee, similar to how one might pay $70 a month for cable or $15 a month to stream Apple Music or Netflix.
- It could be that you pay per trip.
- Or it could be some combination of both — for $50 you get access to a certain tier of cars *and* you pay $3 a mile.

Autonomous vehicles are today seen mostly as a solution for cities.

"Outside urban areas, the personal car will be king. I don't see an Uber getting to price parity in rural areas," says Clark.

Consulting firm OC&C found that 82% of consumers in the U.S. and Europe still want exclusive use of a car — autonomous or otherwise. But the smaller percentage of drivers who would be willing to consider sharing their vehicle is growing. In 2021, it was 14%, nearly double the 2019 number of just 8%.

When Level 4 and Level 5 autonomy is eventually adopted, 30% to 40% of drivers report that they "would not mind" using a pool of autonomous cars rather than having their own.

Part of the still small number of consumers willing to consider a self-driving car is due to lack of familiarity. But there's also cost.

OC&C found that just 15% of drivers would spend $2,500 extra for a fully autonomous vehicle. For aftermarket upgrades, OC&C reports that only 23% of so-called "early adopters" would pay an extra $1,000 for the lidar and other equipment required to make a car self-driving.

The one curveball in this analysis: The lingering effects of COVID-19, which pushed consumers away from public transportation into private vehicles, where the risk of contagion is less. Will that "muscle memory" of avoiding public spaces influence the buy versus share equation when self-driving cars become a widespread reality in another twenty or thirty years, such that consumers will want a vehicle for their own exclusive use?

Or will new sterilizing and air-purification technology become available that may make a shared autonomous vehicle, counterintuitively, one of the *safest* places to be in a pandemic?

THE FUTURE IS HYBRID

Automotive industry consultant Ed French believes the future will be a hybrid.

"There will be a core group of humans that continue to want to drive their cars," he told me. "Autonomous vehicles and human-driven vehicles will coexist seamlessly for the next thirty years. I don't think I could ever envision the 16-year-olds of today just getting in the vehicle and not letting them experience driving a vehicle."

Glenn Mercer says we will definitely see some autonomous vehicles individually owned rather than belonging to a fleet or a ride-sharing provider. "If I like the Mercedes S-Class [as a non-autonomous vehicle],

I'll be happy to spend $20,000 more to get the self-driving version," he told me.

French envisions a car "where the autonomy can be switched on and off" as needed based on driving (and driver) conditions.

Jay Vijayan of Tekion says the biggest hurdle to autonomy is that the vehicles need to talk to the public infrastructure — traffic lights and the like — not to mention to each other.

"The last mile may take longer than all the progress that's happened so far," he told me. "The last 5% is the hardest."

"I'm certain we won't have any Level 5 cars in our lifetime!" Reilly Brennan predicted in a conversation we had recently. He's more bullish on Level 4. "If a robot tells you that you shouldn't be driving in zero-visibility weather in February near Chicago, it won't do it. So, by definition, it becomes Level 4 rather than Level 5."

Brennan believes we may never have true Level 5 cars.

"Only humans are dumb enough to think they should be driving in every condition possible, whereas machines are much smarter than that."

This inability of autonomous vehicles to operate in inclement weather is one of the reasons most of the current trials are being conducted in locations with notably sunny weather, like Arizona and Silicon Valley, where confounding variables — rain, fog, dirt, salt and dust — are less likely to interfere with the smooth operation of all those sensors on the vehicle. If a car starts to slide around in the snow, that's a complex interaction, and the autonomous driving system may not understand what's going on.

Seen in that light, Tesla's Autopilot is terrible branding, Brennan says. "It lulls some drivers into believing it's autonomous." That may improve as Tesla rolls out FSD — its "Full Self-Driving" suite — a paid add-on that bolts additional services onto Autopilot but which the *New York Times* says is "not quite" full self-driving.

GM has a monitoring system in some of its cars that looks to see if drivers are paying attention and not reading the newspaper or falling asleep, Brennan notes. "If they are, it turns off the system."

CHAPTER SIX   127

When (and if) Level 5 becomes a reality, will regulations ultimately ban human drivers?

Amnon Shashua would certainly advocate for that, although it may happen in countries like France or Norway way before it takes root in the U.S.

Brennan doesn't disagree with Shashua. "But humans probably won't be allowed to drive without some monitoring of their activities," he admits.

Whether it's humans with monitoring or no driver at all, autonomy is inevitable if it can reduce fatalities. Why have a fallible human behind the wheel of a car when computers make far fewer mistakes?

Indeed, robots are replacing people wherever there's high-risk activity. The same is true with coal mining, metal smelting, assembly lines and the handling of uranium in nuclear power plants.

Putting aside those concerns of a Terminator/SkyNet future, when robots take over, deaths and injuries wane.

We're already seeing that in the air: Some 90% of commercial airline pilots use their planes' autopilot systems. That's made flying safer (do you really want a pilot who didn't sleep well the night before clutching the steering wheel the entire flight?) but led to other concerns. Are pilots losing their manual flying skills and would thus be less able to respond to a hands-on emergency?

Will the same be true for self-driving cars?

For that matter, if cars existed when the Founding Fathers were framing the U.S. constitution, would Jefferson, Washington, Franklin et al., have included "the right to drive your own car" in the list of preambles? Or would they have nixed that option in favor of safety and convenience?

If a municipality allows only certain license plates to enter the city center on certain days of the week (as is already the case in cities such as Shanghai and London), would autonomous vehicles be exempt?

Cliff Banks, automotive industry analyst and editor of the *Banks Report,* says the future is difficult to discern.

"We've had one hundred years of knowing what a vehicle looks like, what kind of propulsion system it has, how the retail and distribution system works," he told me. "Today, nothing much has changed. Cars got bigger and better, but in 1915, one of the bestselling models was a Ford pickup truck. Today, it's still a pickup truck."

PRESSURE ON DEALERS

One thing is for sure: When autonomy becomes more widespread, a sizable proportion of autonomous vehicles will be shared or subscribed to from a fleet operator. The result will be far fewer cars sold and even more pressure on dealers to find ways to make up the revenue in other areas, such as service (autonomous vehicles, with all their sensors and embedded gizmos, will need qualified professionals and OEM-endorsed equipment to take care of them when they break down).

Autonomy by subscription will also favor the OEM or fleet owner over the dealer. After all, if you're paying a monthly fee and the car just shows up, you don't need a relationship with a dealer at all. Your relationship is with Toyota or Hertz. It's another reason autonomy is so potentially hazardous to dealers.

So, should autonomy be top of mind for dealers today?

Probably not.

Today's Levels 1, 2 and 3 won't move the needle all that much. If anything, these more complex vehicles will mean more service work for dealers — repairing, replacing and calibrating the sophisticated camera, lidar and radar systems embedded in self-driving cars.

But in the long term, autonomy threatens to be pretty disruptive to both vehicle sales and service. Dealers should start preparing to accommodate these changes. My advice: Put in place a forward-looking plan sooner rather than later.

In years to come, will young people look at their aging parents in disbelief when they're told that "people used to drive cars," as Larry Burns suggests?

Tesla CEO Elon Musk said early in 2021 that he was "highly confident [a Tesla autonomous vehicle] will be able to drive itself with a reliability in excess of humans this year." Musk may have gotten a bit ahead of himself, but the excitement is palpable — even if for the moment the future remains largely uncertain.

Banks says that when he's preparing a presentation, he will sometimes display a photo showing automotive industry executives in front of a curved road. The point is to demonstrate how "they couldn't see beyond the curve. That's similar to the way we just don't know what the future will look like."

The first self-driving experiment dates back to 1977 when Tokyo-based Tsukuba Mechanical pioneered a driverless car that could achieve speeds of nearly 20 miles per hour.

That experiment fizzled, leading Shashua to comment, "In this field, being first isn't all that critical. I think we'll be among the first, and also that the number of players who will be able to come up with a quality autonomous car that will pass regulation will be very small — fewer than you can count on the fingers of one hand. It's an investment of billions. The technology required is no less than what's required to send a person to Mars. A small company that works for a year or two can't achieve the necessary scale of activity and degree of precision."

Late in 2021, Intel announced that it plans to take Mobileye public in mid-2022. Will capital from the public markets enable the company to reach its destination?

CHAPTER SEVEN

THE CONNECTED CAR

"There are so many growth opportunities we have. Think about the vehicle not only as an electric vehicle, but as a software platform."
— **Mary Barra, CEO of General Motors**

In 2013, a Tesla Model S caught fire after it ran over a piece of debris in the road, which apparently punctured or dented the car's battery pack. In response, Tesla pushed an over-the-air (OTA) update to all its Model S vehicles that raised the car's ride height when it hit highway speeds.

Tesla CEO Elon Musk insisted at the time that the update to the vehicle's suspension system was "about reducing the chances of underbody impact damage, not improving safety," but the real importance was how it demonstrated the power of the connected car.

When Consumer Reports discovered in 2018 that braking distance on the Tesla Model 3 was worse than that of a (nonelectric) Ford F-150, an OTA update improved the vehicle's stopping range by 19 feet, prompting the article's author, Jake Fisher, to comment with amazement that he'd "never seen a car that could improve its track performance with an over-the-air update."

Today's new cars are essentially laptops on wheels, always connected to the network wirelessly and thus able to update their operating systems, as with a computer or a mobile device, without having to visit to a physical repair shop.

And computers they are.

Bosch reports that new cars have over one hundred million lines of software code. McKinsey suggests that will double in the coming years to three hundred million. That's on top of the three thousand semiconductors in the average modern vehicle.

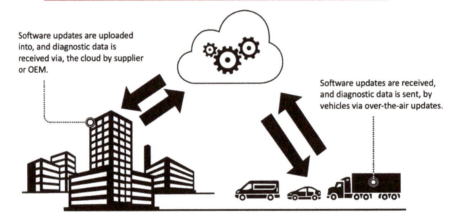

OTA updates can take place overnight via Wi-Fi or using a cellular signal. Between telematics and driving behavior transmitted to the OEM, connected cars generate some 25 gigabytes of data per hour.

The ability to improve how a vehicle performs long after it leaves the sales floor was unheard of before Tesla. Now it's becoming commonplace.

- Ford has built OTA updates into its Mustang Mach-E and electric F-150 pickup truck. The company says it expects to have thirty-three million OTA-capable vehicles on the roads by 2028. The Ford+ subscription service will include updates to its BlueCruise hands-free driver-assist software. "'Always-on' means we are regularly interacting with our customers on things large and small, and we're building new capabilities like connected services to enrich the customer experience and drive recurring revenue streams," Ford CEO Jim Farley told *Automotive News*.
- Porsche's Mission E will offer OTA updates too, with Porsche chairman Oliver Blume giving the example of a 400-horsepower vehicle that could be upgraded over the air to 450 horsepower.
- Mercedes-Benz says 1.3 million vehicles could avoid a dealership visit to repair a communications module if the driver subscribes to the company's "Mercedes me" service, which includes OTA updates.
- BMW charges $220 for an OTA update that allows drivers to dim their headlights so they don't blind others. It's part of BMW's "High Beam Assistant" package.

Tesla, meanwhile, has continued its policy of over-the-air updates, pushing out new adaptive suspension settings for its Model S and Model X Raven vehicles that enable the car to automatically raise itself up in snow, on a steep driveway or wherever a higher ride will improve the car's performance.

Other OTA updates from Tesla alert drivers if they've left their car with a window, door or trunk still open; add additional functionality to Tesla's Powerwall home backup batteries; unlock a 5% power increase; and improve braking, range and autonomous features.

Tesla's Full Self-Driving (FSD) system, for example, will be delivered to customers OTA for between $99 and $199 a month depending on the vehicle, versus buying it upfront for $10,000.

Smart Summon, a Tesla feature that drives your car to you (particularly useful in an unwieldy parking garage) and the video game Caraoke have been delivered OTA.

From 2017 through 2020, more than 120 OTA updates were delivered to the Tesla Model 3 alone, according to Teslarati, a popular Tesla review site.

IHS Markit Automotive estimates that the total cost savings for OEMs from OTA updates will be $35 billion in 2022 (up from $2.7 billion in 2015).

ABI Research estimated in 2015 that, of the $18 billion manufacturers spent on warranty work, some $6 billion could have been saved if OTA updates were available at the time.

Source: ABI Research

Here's what else an OTA update can do:

- Add upgraded features and equipment as a car ages.
- Deliver new services, increasing potential recurring revenue opportunities.
- Improve the car's handling and power.
- Add temporary functionality. Would you like four-wheel drive in the winter but not in the summer? Going on a family road trip and want to add live TV to the seatback screens? Press a button

and pay a small fee, and the kiddies will be entertained for the duration of the ride.

I wouldn't be surprised if, in the future, you'll be able to change the color of your car through an OTA update.

As new rules and regulations are introduced — whether for fuel efficiency or autonomous driving — OTA updates will likely address those issues.

Some 86% of consumers say they would be willing to pay more for a product in exchange for great customer service, notes Brian Benstock, partner, general manager and vice president of Paragon Auto Group, a leading Honda and Acura dealer in Queens, New York.

What could be more customer-friendly than getting your new service delivered without leaving home — or your car, for that matter?

BY THE NUMBERS

McKinsey, in a report titled *Unlocking the Full Life-Cycle Value from Connected-Car Data,* estimates that the overall revenue pool from car data monetization could reach $750 billion by 2030. On a per-vehicle level, this equates to $310 in revenue and $180 in cost savings per year.

The consulting group also says that, in the same period, 95% of new vehicles sold globally will be connected, up from about 50% today.

Ben Volkow, CEO of connected car ecosystem vendor Otonomo, says we should reach the 95% figure even faster, by 2027.

ABI Research forecasts nearly 203 million OTA-enabled cars will ship by 2022. In the U.S., 91% of new vehicles will be connected, compared with 51% in Asia-Pacific and 37% in Latin America.

Consulting firm SBD Automotive says that 70% of cars sold in European markets in 2020 were connected.

Guidehouse Insights market intelligence firm predicts that by 2028, "more than 117 million vehicles sold annually will be capable of supporting OTA updates of most systems inside the vehicle."

OTA updates are still far from perfect. In 2018, for example, users of Fiat Chrysler's Uconnect system discovered, after an OTA update, that their entertainment and navigation systems would reboot every forty-five seconds, during which time drivers couldn't listen to the radio or use the GPS or even the rear-facing camera in the car.

Glitches aside, it is increasingly certain that drivers will be able to pay to unlock features such as increased battery range or an enhanced in-cabin experience for a small one-time payment or an ongoing monthly fee.

WHO GETS THE REVENUE?

This is perhaps the most important question about OTA updates.

If an update is pushed out by an OEM, it stands to reason that the manufacturer would collect any new online subscription fees.

Dealers will want in, but will the OEMs be willing to share?

The OEMs can easily make the argument that they built the car, they built the software and they developed the code for the new product feature, so the revenue should be theirs exclusively.

Dealers, on the other hand, will say that if they sold a car, they deserve the opportunity to continue the relationship through service and upsells. Dealers want to ensure that car owners come back to *them* rather than visit the nearest Jiffy Lube.

The OEMs, in some cases, may not be sympathetic to this argument, although at least one OEM, Audi, says it plans to share revenue with dealers, explained John Newman, head of digitization at the company.

"What we want to look for are opportunities for dealers to bring new sources of value to the customer, and in that sense, absolutely, we are committed to share the revenue and share the profitability of these opportunities with our dealers," he says.

Audi's approach makes sense to me, and I imagine that, despite the typical tug-of-war dynamics between dealers and OEMs, manufacturers will ultimately feel compelled to share revenue, both to protect dealer margins and to ensure that questions consumers have about their new OTA-updated service can be answered by a local expert rather than a faraway OEM customer help desk.

The Banks Report's Cliff Banks believes OEMs will have no choice but to work in partnership with dealers.

"From a diagnostic point of view, the OEMs will need that data," Banks told me. "The OEMs will then determine to which dealership the data goes. But it's the OEMs that will dictate the price and which dealer gets the referral." That could even result in an auction scenario where dealers compete against each other.

"Dealers will have to play ball if they want a piece of the game," Banks says.

Dennis Clark, formerly of Honda Innovations, doesn't believe an auction model will come to pass.

"Having an unknown dealer or service center pop up randomly on your car's screen [if it's the auction winner] is not conducive to an OEM's brand," he told me. "It's more likely that the system will recommend the closest dealer or one where the customer already has a relationship."

A McKinsey report found that 58% of customers in the U.S., China, Brazil and Germany would follow their vehicle's recommendation of a repair shop or dealer.

What if the behind-the-scenes "auction" software recommends a dealer where the driver previously had a bad experience? wonders Jay Vijayan of Tekion. In that case, users must be able to choose another, he suggests. If drivers have the option to rate their dealer experience, the software should remember the ranking and not serve up an inappropriate recommendation the second time around.

Smart dealers will get ahead of this by sending out a survey immediately after a service visit.

"The customer experience needs to be measured in real time," notes Vijayan. "The system needs to show all interactions so the dealer has the opportunity to correct it. Just going to Yelp or Google Reviews and typing in how bad the visit was will have to change. When a negative experience is turned into a positive one, consumers will stay a long time."

Any kind of auction/recommendation engine, even behind the scenes, will have to minimize decision paralysis. No one wants to receive inquiries from seventeen different Toyota dealers in Atlanta about a possible repair. Just present the top choice and give the driver the ability to drill down if he or she wishes. (Most people will go with the easiest option.)

Vijayan says consumers must be given some choice, whether that's the last place they visited, the dealership where they bought their car or the closest dealer. "The consumer must be in control," he stresses.

APPLECARE FOR CARS

Ultimately, Vijayan believes that recurring subscriptions — like AppleCare for computers, iPhones and tablets — also make sense for connected cars.

"Tech companies are killing it with subscriptions," he notes. "Apple, Google and so many services are just easy to purchase. I don't use them half the time. For example, I have three different backup services. But people will pay for peace of mind, for preventative care."

Vijayan would like to see a rating and recommendation engine for connected cars and services, like "the way Amazon says '80% of consumers who bought this also bought that.'"

Is there a magic price point?

- Vijayan suggests $9.99 to $14.99 a month depending on the services offered — the Amazon, Netflix or Apple model. "People won't mind paying for something they feel good about, even if they may not need it all the time." What will turn off consumers? "Services where they feel they're being pushed to spend. That needs to change."
- Tesla already charges $9.99 a month for a "premium connectivity" plan that includes OTA updates. (Any new Tesla

with a premium interior includes a year of free premium connectivity; a basic connectivity package that includes maps and navigation tools remains free.)
- A premium subscription to GM's OnStar connectivity plan runs significantly more, at $25 a month, and is required if users want to receive Super Cruise maps and hands-free driving. (GM also offers an unlimited data plan without Super Cruise for the same price.) Super Cruise will be available in twenty-two GM models by 2023; it's already in the Cadillac Escalade and Chevy Bolt.
- The data plan that comes with the Volkswagen ID.4 electric vehicle is free — but only for the first month. After that, subscribers pay $20 each month for a Verizon mobile data plan.
- The NissanConnect service has four different price points, ranging from $8.00 to $12.99 a month. It includes remote door locking, a vehicle health report, maintenance notifications, OTA updates, and map and traffic features. Nissan's ProPilot Assist, an advanced driver assistance system like Tesla's Autopilot, is included in the price of its high-end vehicles with no monthly fee.

What's behind the pricing? Aurora Labs lays out four cost considerations in a white paper titled *Automotive Over-the-Air Updates: A Cost Consideration Guide*:

1. Data transmission costs for cloud-to-vehicle communication — that is, the cost for sending updates via cellular services.
2. Cloud storage costs — how much do cloud storage providers charge to hold onto the files that will be transmitted via the OTA update?
3. Endpoint update and technology integration costs — this is what's required to enable a car to receive an OTA update. Development can run up to $1.5 million per model.
4. Incremental cost of dual bank storage — this is necessary to avoid drawing down the car's battery.

These costs are not insignificant; if an OEM sells ten million vehicles that all require an OTA update, the annual data transmission cost can easily reach into the hundreds of millions of dollars, Aurora points out. 5G cellular networks could bring this cost down, but that must be balanced by an increasing volume of OTA updates.

McKinsey estimates that consumers will be willing to pay about $13 a month for advanced map features and personalized navigation, or for fuel- and cost-efficiency features.

"Are you willing to pay $2 so the car finds you a parking spot instead of circling around for half an hour to find it yourself?" asks Axel Schmidt, head of global automotive at the consulting firm Accenture.

How about $10 to add sound isolation, where you can be in a vehicle with other people and you can't hear them, only your own music or voice calls?

Would you pay that amount for what Giovanni Lanfranchi, chief technology officer of digital mapping company HERE Technologies, describes as a competitor to Waze "that uses car-to-car communication to predict traffic situations just five minutes ahead using AI and machine learning to achieve up to 95% accuracy?"

I know I would!

GM'S BOLD PLAY

General Motors told investors in October 2021 that it expected its in-car subscription services to generate more than $2 billion in revenue that year, reaching as high as $25 billion by the end of the decade. That would put it in the same league as Netflix, Peloton and Spotify in terms of subscription revenue, the company noted.

GM has some sixteen million vehicles on the road in the U.S. and Canada. About a quarter of those vehicles — 4.2 million — already have owners paying for subscription services, mainly through GM's OnStar service, Alan Wexler, the company's senior vice-president of innovation and growth, said at a company investor event. He expects that number to grow further when GM's Ultifi software platform launches in 2023.

Ultifi looks poised to be in the right place at the right time: It enables the frequent and seamless delivery of features and services to customers over the air.

"Today, cars are enabled by software. With Ultifi, they are going to be defined by it," says Scott Miller, GM vice president for software-defined vehicles.

Ultifi builds on GM's electric vehicle architecture, called the Vehicle Intelligence Platform, although the service will be available for both electric and gas-powered cars.

Miller likes to emphasize the safety aspects of Ultifi, which he calls "profound." These include:

- Internal cameras used for facial recognition to start the vehicle.
- Automatic closing of a sunroof in a parked car if rain is in the forecast.
- Automatically turning on the child locks when children are sensed in the back seat.

Once Ultifi is up and running, Wexler predicts that "with the right mix of compelling offerings, customers [will be] willing to spend $135 per month on average for products and services."

GM surveyed its customers and found that a typical subscription bundle could include up to twenty-five products and services.

Tops on GM's list:

- Super Cruise enhancements
- In-vehicle personalization themes
- Over-the-air navigation
- Parking assistance
- Insights on fleet vehicles (for commercial customers)

If, as GM forecasts, thirty million of the company's vehicles in the U.S. will have some form of connected car technology by 2030, that will result in an addressable market of $80 billion, with GM aiming to generate additional incremental revenue of $20 billion to $25 billion.

Some $6 billion of that will be from usage-based insurance and the rest from one-time purchases and recurring subscriptions.

GM's OnStar costs between $25 and $50 a month, or $2,000 as a standalone option. It has operating margins of more than 70%.

"Hundreds of thousands of connected fleet vehicles with data from millions of trips and hundreds of millions of miles — all of that data provides huge monetization opportunities," Wexler notes.

Keep in mind the Gillette business model, where the company essentially gives away the razor handle while making money by selling disposable blades. Similarly, in the automotive space, the sale of the vehicle may not be where the money is made, but there should be enough margin on subscription services to share healthy profits with both OEMs and dealers.

"The way we interact with our vehicle is going to be very different as this migration, this transformation, continues to happen," GM CFO Paul Jacobson says. "We see it as something that's a good baseline for more to come as customers get more comfortable with that subscription service and the value that they want to purchase through the vehicle."

VEHICLE RECALLS

OTA updates result in significant savings for an automaker in terms of labor costs.

Recalls are costly and time-consuming. It can take months for dealers to schedule all customers impacted. By contrast, an OTA update requires only a few minutes to complete — a huge convenience and savings.

OTA updates can also increase the chances of repairing more or even all of the vehicles covered by a recall.

That's not an insignificant problem:

RECALLS ARE A SIGNIFICANT PROBLEM

63 million
Number of vehicles with open safety recalls.

31 million
Number of vehicles recalled in 2020.

$500
Average cost of an automotive recall over the last ten years.

~70%
The percent of recalls that are ultimately completed. (NHTSA)

While consumers and automakers win with OTA updates around recalls, once again it's the dealers who will bear the brunt of the changes if recall work migrates away from the repair shop in favor of updating online. Dealers will miss the profit margin (guaranteed by the OEM) on the recall repair, the ability to upsell additional work to the consumer and the opportunity to engender brand loyalty through the additional touchpoint with their customer.

"Car dealers have everything to lose," says Susan Beardslee, a senior analyst at ABI Research. "When the automotive industry becomes fully OTA, car dealers lose not only the revenue enhancement that they acquire in making updates and repairs, but they lose the associated foot traffic."

THE CONNECTED CAR KNOWS WHERE YOU'VE BEEN (AND WHERE YOU'LL GO NEXT)

I've focused so far in this chapter on the ability of OTA updates to improve a car's performance and operation. But the same always-connected functionality that makes OTA updates possible also means your car can be personalized in ways never before imagined.

By communicating with an OEM's centralized server, your car will know your usual commuting route, whether and where you stop for your morning brew, where you plug in to charge your electric vehicle, your kids' and spouse's birthdays (and what types of chocolate or flowers they favor), medicines you regularly take (plus where and when to refill prescriptions), what music, news or podcasts you enjoy on your way to work and much more.

Just like with auctions between dealers, connected cars could spark battles behind the scenes between retailers. If you're a regular Starbucks customer, for example, could you be swayed by an in-dash coupon for a free cuppa at Dunkin' or Peet's?

Would you pay extra for a no-ad interface (much like you can bypass the ads in Spotify or YouTube with a premium subscription)?

Will the smart audio interface in your car be custom-built by the OEM, or will Amazon or Apple cut deals with manufacturers to integrate Alexa or Siri more tightly into the car's operation, making it your default personal assistant across devices and brands?

The latter seems a good possibility: Amazon has already made its Alexa technology available for carmakers to build custom assistants. So far, a dozen brands, including Audi, BMW, Buick, Cadillac, Chevrolet, Ford, GM, Lincoln, Lexus and Toyota are on board.

One way to incentivize connected car data use is to deliver a sticky, impossible-to-ignore prompt.

What if, every morning, when you got into your car, your dashboard displayed the vehicle's current trade-in value?

If your car is a lease, Toyota could delight you by offering a brand-new car at a lower monthly payment as your Prius lease period is coming to an end.

What if you know you need snow tires for the winter but it's still summer? An update would let you know when prices are rising and it's time to bite the bullet, even when it's 100 degrees outside and snow is a few months away. Throw in a free driveway tire change, and it's a no-brainer.

OEMs may want to build their own connectivity services, but as with vehicle entertainment systems, proprietary interfaces are giving way to Apple CarPlay and Android Auto.

My take: It's probably best for the OEMs to leave the heavy lifting to the Silicon Valley giants that have greater experience with interface design and artificial intelligence. (Or acquire a startup!)

SCREENS, SCREENS EVERYWHERE

When connected cars intersect with autonomy, the car's interior may be transformed into one large screen (or screens) — for entertainment, for work, for navigation, for shopping.

- Will your car read your emails to you while you're commuting?
- Will it remind you that it's your wedding anniversary tonight and ask if you would like to make restaurant reservations at that little place you liked so much last year?
- Would you prefer the yellow roses again or something different this time?
- What's on your calendar for the rest of the week?

It sounds creepy and privacy infringing — and any time data about your life is being aggregated, there's always that possibility — but the aim is to make your life easier and more efficient the more your car (and all your devices, for that matter) knows about your habits and preferences.

Connected-car advocates want to transform your car from a tool into a true partner that understands you intimately.

Have you been slacking off at the gym? Your car can block off an hour for you tonight if you're willing (and have packed your Lululemon yoga pants in the trunk — which your car will prompt you to remember for next time).

THE CONNECTED CAR IN ACTION

Cliff Banks describes how he imagines a connected car could interact with passengers.

"Let's say I'm on my way out of town for a work meeting. I get into my car, which is already warmed up. I use the remote start app from my phone. The steering wheel and seats are already heated. The car greets me, 'Welcome back, Cliff. Traffic to the airport is light. And by the way, you'll need new brakes or work on your transmission in about a month. ABC Brakes has a slot open in three days. Would you like me to set an appointment? Would you prefer to bring me to the dealer or have me picked up at your home? Will you need a loaner car or a ride home?'"

The point is, according to Banks, "It's not the dealer or the manufacturer telling me I need new brakes. It's the car."

Nemodata is doing something similar with trucks and delivery vehicles.

The company's AI software allows fleet owners, such as Amazon or UPS, to schedule preventative maintenance *before* the vehicle fails. The American Trucking Associations reports that Class 8 trucks experience a roadside breakdown *every 10,000 miles*, costing fleets more than $5,000 per truck per year.

Fewer emergency repairs can increase a fleet's uptime by five days per truck annually, the association says. And by reducing engine, tire and brake failures, drivers can feel more confident they're helming a safe vehicle.

Indeed, every time someone presses a button or swipes on a touchscreen in a connected car or truck, feedback should be recorded that can help manufacturers improve their vehicles' interfaces going forward. If they see that drivers always need to monkey around with the temperature controls or that it takes a long time to fumble through the radio stations, it's worth stepping back to figure out how to make those more user-friendly.

Take the case of heated headlights.

These work by defrosting any snow that has accumulated on them. But how many drivers actually know how to use that feature?

How many don't even know it exists because they weren't onboarded properly?

Today, there's no way to know that, say, only 17% of people who buy heated headlamps use them. In the future, OEMs will have that data broken down by geography, demographics and more. The car could prompt the driver — "Hey, it's winter, and you haven't used your heated headlights yet" — or charge an additional fee to "unlock" this functionality as needed. If drivers in Boston use the heated headlights option a lot, maybe the OEM can increase the price come the following winter, driving higher profits in Massachusetts but not in Mississippi.

If a connected car relies on drivers synching up their phones with their cars, and it's been a month since the last sync, that tells the OEM that there must be a problem. Maybe there's a new phone in the family or the sync software is malfunctioning and the driver doesn't know how to fix it.

The OEM or dealer could reach out proactively: "We'd be happy to send someone to your driveway to help."

Or maybe the problem is serious but hidden.

If the connected car detects a wiring bug, it could alert drivers. "You need to get your electrical cables changed; otherwise, they could spark a fire in your garage."

That would get my attention fast!

McKinsey found that 39% of customers would appreciate the ability to unlock additional features after purchasing their vehicle, rather than having to make those decisions before leaving the dealer's lot. In the premium segment, this number rises to 47%. (And in China, it's even higher, at 63%.)

By monitoring how people use their cars, dealers can delight, build trust and better retain their most valuable asset: their customers.

THE CONNECTED CAR TIMELINE

How soon will all this play out? Maniv Mobility investor Mike Granoff isn't sure.

"Data has been hyped to death over the last couple of years — vehicle data in particular," he told me. "It may take longer to happen than we first thought."

Granoff suggests a few use cases for the connected car.

"Starbucks anticipating when you'll arrive. Traffic patterns shared with financial institutions. Microclimates based on the internal temperature in the cabin and whether the wipers are on. Delivery to a car's trunk, where the connected software pops the hood automatically."

Reilly Brennan, general partner of Trucks Venture Capital, questions whether we need to imbue our cars with so many smarts.

"What needs to be on your car versus on your phone?" he wonders. "If the car needs maintenance, we could show you something on the car's display and present a route to the dealership. Other things, like purchases at Starbucks, are more closely attached to the user and so should stay on the device — the phone or smartwatch. When I look at startups that claim they will do payments in the vehicle, well, the list is pretty thin: parking, tolls and that's about it. Most things should remain on the device."

Brennan's point: Does your car really need your credit card information? How important is it to prepay for that Egg McMuffin rather than whip out your phone and use Apple Pay?

Still, most of the VCs and analysts I spoke to say connectivity is coming.

"I'd put my money on the Internet of Things for cars that can self-diagnose a failure or find a pizza at a discount," Bill Cariss of Holman Strategic Ventures told me.

WHAT KIND OF DATA IS BEING COLLECTED?

Connected cars collect a wide variety of information:

- Vehicle (technical and performance) data
- Driver data (is the driver falling asleep at the wheel?)
- Location data (real-time or saved information about favorite

destinations)
- 🚗 Data about the surroundings (distance between cars, potholes, traffic signs)

Tactile Mobility is a leading player in the latter case; the company equips municipal service cars (such as parking-enforcement vehicles) to collect data about the roads on which they travel.

Tactile can tell through the sensors already installed in cars that control steering and braking how tightly a car is gripping the road (which could indicate slippery conditions), whether the car is bumping up and down (as it travels over potholes) and how steep a hill is.

That data is then shared with the city to provide "actionable insights" that can be used to identify areas in need of quick repair.

Further down the road, so to speak, this will make it easier for self-driving cars to handle difficult-to-navigate highway on- and off-ramps.

In another pilot, Argo AI and Rapid Flow Technologies teamed up in 2020 for a project where data from connected cars communicate with traffic lights. Rapid Flow had already generated encouraging results on its own: Traffic delays dropped by as much as 20%, and travel times decreased by 16%. When Argo's self-driving cars were added to the mix, the time spent sitting at red lights was cut by some 40%, the companies reported.

PRIVACY CONCERNS

The connected cars of the future will have the same kinds of privacy concerns that regulators are concerned about for our computers and phones today. The key question: How much does the car need to know about you? Does it really need to know when you last went to the gym or what groceries you most recently bought?

Companies like Otonomo are building a marketplace for this kind of vehicle data. The Israeli startup (which went public in 2021 through a SPAC merger that valued the company at $1.26 billion) has built an ecosystem for sharing driving data with third-party companies, fleet managers and OEMs.

The data is intended to improve the functioning of smart cities, creating greater access for emergency services, providing data to help decide where to locate EV charge points, solving parking problems and enabling predictive maintenance. Data also leads to better traffic management and mapping.

Otonomo's partners include BMW, Daimler and Mitsubishi.

Mercedes-Benz, another Otonomo customer, collects data on fuel or charging, vehicle status (are the doors locked, lights off, sunroof closed?) and insurance (where it supports "pay-as-you-drive" pricing based on odometer readings and time stamps).

Will others come on board? Or is there an inherent conflict of interest between Otonomo, which is gunning for an entirely open market, and the OEMs, which will want to run their own closed, walled-off gardens?

Building the Otonomo ecosystem is not trivial. It requires commercial agreements and integration with each OEM separately. Any data needs to be normalized since OEMs store data in different formats. Anonymization, auditing, billing and management add to the complexity.

"Building a connected car service today is much more difficult than providing applications before the smartphone days," writes Amit Karp of Bessemer Venture Partners, which invested in Otonomo. "The solution to this will either be a common car operating system — unlikely given the OEM's fear of the tech giants — or a third-party platform that simplifies launching connected car services."

Progressive Insurance's Snapshot service is a good example of the pay-as-you-go insurance concept.

After you download the Snapshot app, it monitors your driving for thirty days, then offers you a price quote. If you drive more aggressively, tailgate and go around corners faster, you will likely be ranked as more of a risk (and therefore deserving of higher rates) than someone who never exceeds the speed limit.

The app monitors how many times you had to hard brake and whether you drive late at night (uh-oh, your rates just went up). Good drivers save on average around $146 a year, the company says.

Insurance apps like Progressive's are becoming increasingly common; some are based just on what the app can determine using sensors already built into the phone. Others plug into the onboard diagnostics (OBD2) interface under the dashboard to glean data directly from the car. (OBD2 is a mainstay of internal combustion engine vehicles but is not as relevant for electric cars.)

Will drivers be given the choice to opt-in to Otonomo's services? Or will it come built-in when the car is delivered, with a complicated unsubscribe process buried in the Terms of Service agreement that no one really reads? What incentives will drivers need to be comfortable with how their data is being used?

THE ELEPHANT IN THE ROOM

Then there's the elephant in the room whenever data is mentioned: What happens if your car is hacked — not to disable your brakes in a terror attack, but a more prosaic (and common) kind of hack to steal your shopping preferences and personal information?

OEMs will need to be super careful to anonymize all data that's being sold, ensuring that no names or social security numbers are attached.

There's also another elephant to come: the use of biometric data to unlock and authenticate a car's operations. Will this be a requirement, or will drivers be able to opt out, say, with a physical key instead of a thumbprint or an iris scan?

Already, many cars can automatically unlock when a wirelessly connected keychain is nearby. There are also companies such as CarIQ that go one step further and make it possible to drive up to a gas station and pay for your fuel without having to swipe your credit card or pull out a wad of cash.

DO YOU TRUST ME?

European privacy regulations have always been stricter than those in the U.S., but as Banks told me, "I don't know if the younger generation cares so much. It will be much less of an issue in the U.S. In China, it's not even a conversation."

In December 2019 and January 2020, consulting firm SBD Automotive conducted a survey of 2,500 recent model (2016 or newer) car owners in France, Germany, Italy, Spain and the U.K.

Among the findings:

- Up to 71% of those who expressed interest in connected car services would be willing to share data specific to their cars, although the percentage drops off for services related to convenience rather than safety. (Alerts on dangerous driving conditions were top ranked; on-demand car washes came in much lower.)
- 80% said they would consider sharing data if they received an incentive. Top incentives include cheaper car insurance, discounts on servicing, longer warranty periods and ways to prevent breakdowns.
- More than half of European consumers are OK with sharing anonymized data.
- Awareness about the car data collected by OEMs is low; only 59% of consumers said they know that data from cars can be shared with manufacturers.
- 60% of respondents said it's very important to be told exactly what data is being collected, how it is being used and by whom.
- 59% said the trustworthiness of the company or app is very important.
- 75% want to see the car data they are sharing.
- Drivers from the U.K. and Italy were the most willing to share their data, while German consumers were the most reluctant.

If your car knows that you leave for daycare pickup every day at 3 p.m., and it can integrate with your calendar to schedule maintenance while avoiding a scheduling conflict, you might be less averse to relinquishing some privacy, especially if you trust the source of the app.

After all, you don't think twice about doing this with traffic apps such as Waze, which can sense that at 8:30 a.m., you're most likely going to work and will suggest your office address as the top search destination.

Let's say your car has just run over a nail. If your vehicle can alert you the second after the spike encounter that you're going to have a problem, rather than waiting for the tire to begin deflating later in the day, you'll be more willing to share. You don't have to answer a dozen questions on the phone, either; the car will have already informed the dealer or repair shop that there's a nail problem and that within the next three hours, your tire will be flat.

A message reading, "Unless you put air in your tires today, there's a 77% chance the tire will blow" or "Your battery is discharging faster than it should; let's get you an update" is a strong call to action. It may even engender greater loyalty to the dealer or OEM.

Does it inspire confidence or generate annoyance when you get a call from your insurance company after you've stopped short on the highway to avoid an accident? The company just wants to know you're OK, but it's a reminder that you're being monitored 24/7 whenever you're in your car.

GM's OnStar subsidiary is programmed to call you over the car's speakerphone automatically if it detects your airbags have inflated. If it can't reach you, the next call is to emergency services. Cars with driver monitoring sensors will be able to update the ambulance crew, before they even arrive, on the status of your blood pressure and whether you're having difficulty breathing.

What about sensors that remind you that you've left something in the back seat — a pet or a baby? It's hard to argue with the usefulness of that. (No one really complains anymore when their car dings because a seat belt is not fastened.) Once again, happy to share.

And yet trust remains a concern, especially since dealers consistently rank among the lowest trusted professionals in a consumer's life. (That's one of the reasons I predict that it will be the OEMs who control the connected car relationship.)

Among the reasons drivers don't want to share vehicle data are the following, according to SBD:

- "I don't trust companies to keep my data safe." (75%)
- "I don't want to become a victim of identity theft." (54%)
- "I don't want to be profiled." (43%)

OEMs, perhaps surprisingly, actually enjoy a *high level* of trust among consumers, according to SBD's survey — on a par with consumer trust in credit card companies (which have the capability to detect fraud almost instantly in many cases and thus rank highest on the trust scale).

Sixty-two percent of respondents in Europe were confident that OEMs will properly secure their personal information. In the U.S., it's even higher: 71% trust manufacturers to keep their data safe.

THE COMING STORM

What do I recommend to dealers in the age of the connected car?

It's hard to predict the massive changes that will undoubtedly occur in the next thirty years (autonomy and EV uptake will play a big part in the connectivity story).

In the near term, dealers would do best to stay abreast of what's changing around them, both with the OEMs and the startups in the connected vehicle space.

Above all, I urge you to remain vigilant. Change is always around the corner. Your job is to avoid getting hit by a development that swerves into your blind spot.

"Stakeholders must act fast," write Michele Bertoncello, Christopher Martens, Timo Möller and Tobias Schneiderbauer in the McKinsey report. "New players with innovative approaches could rapidly gain an advantage over slower-moving incumbents. Those that fail to act now will miss the opportunity to differentiate themselves in one of the industry's key customer-facing spaces."

CHAPTER EIGHT

SERVICE AND REPAIRS

> *"Loyal customers, they don't just come back, they don't simply recommend you, they insist that their friends do business with you."*
> — **Chip Bell, Customer Service Consultant**

Jiffy Lube has a problem. The veteran oil change and lube shop, founded in 1971 — and today, with two thousand locations across the U.S. — is facing a future in which electric cars dominate.

What's the issue?

EVs don't use oil, which threatens to decimate Jiffy Lube's core business.

The U.S. oil-change services industry was worth some $8 billion in 2020, according to IBISWorld, and grew an average of 2.4% a year between 2015 and 2020. It employs ninety-three thousand people in nearly thirty thousand stores.

Jiffy Lube is one of ten national chains that account for 60% of those thirty thousand stores. Other oil-focused brands include Valvoline Instant Oil Change and Pennzoil 10-Minute Oil Change. Their "long-term future," writes Loren McDonald for the EVAdoption website, "is certain death unless they pivot along with the shift to electric vehicles."

The story will be much the same for dealerships.

In 2019, franchise dealers generated 49.6% of their gross profits from their service and parts departments, according to the National Automobile Dealers Association (NADA). This critically important profit center is about to change dramatically: Electric vehicles, with fewer moving parts and no need for a lube job, will require less maintenance (other than tires, which seem to wear out faster due to the EV's heavier weight and increased torque).

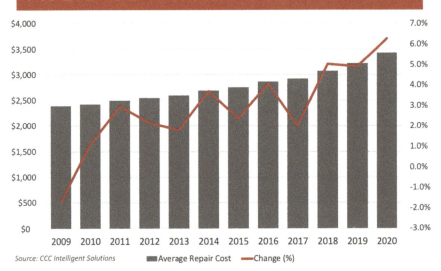

In addition, over-the-air updates, which we explored in the previous chapter, have the potential to further diminish a vehicle's in-store service needs.

When fully autonomous vehicles enter the mix, albeit years from now, the business will change yet again.

To hedge against reduced revenue to their service business, dealers will have to become creative with new offerings, which is the topic we explore in this chapter. The solution may include downsizing — for dealers, the biggest line item is their personnel cost — but there are ample opportunities for additional revenue to mitigate the worst predictions.

Among the new service possibilities dealers could offer are the following:

- Sensor calibration and alignment
- Late-night cleaning and car washes
- Charging spots on the dealer's lot
- Remote/driveway repairs
- Tire sales/subscriptions for EV owners
- EV charging consultation for consumers and commercial customers
- Fleet services
- Online parts e-commerce

THE EV EFFECT

Electric vehicles don't require oil, as they use an electric motor rather than an internal combustion engine, which requires oil to lubricate the valves, pistons and other moving parts so they glide smoothly past each other at high speeds. Oil also enables gasoline-powered engines to operate without seizing or overheating.

After a gas engine is in use for a while, tiny metal flakes accumulate in the oil due to the metal-on-metal contact. These flakes need to be removed, so dealers and dedicated lube shops, such as Jiffy Lube and Pennzoil, drain and add fresh oil to keep the engine running in tip-top shape.

Electric cars, by contrast, have no valves, pistons, engines or moving parts that require lubrication (though they still need some fluids — coolant, windshield washer fluid, brake fluid and transmission fluid).

Moreover, EVs have significantly fewer moving parts: twenty in the drivetrain of an electric car versus close to two thousand for an internal combustion engine vehicle.

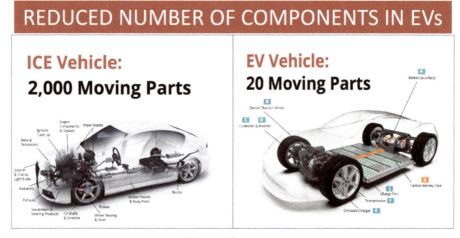

= Fewer parts; less frequent service

Overall, electric vehicles have one-fifth the number of powertrain parts compared with gasoline-powered cars, notes Reilly Brennan of Trucks VC. When combined with the elimination of oil, "the typical automobile will suffer 35% declines in maintenance and service, or roughly $1,300 for an EV versus an internal combustion engine, over a five-year period," he writes in *TechCrunch*.

Oil changes alone account for 24% of all automotive maintenance transactions in the U.S. market.

Brakes need fewer repairs as well, in part because EVs employ a technology known as "regenerative braking," which slows the vehicle down without drivers having to stomp on the brake (you simply lift your foot off the accelerator, and the car not only reduces speed, but also captures kinetic energy that recharges the battery). That results in less wear and tear on the brake pads.

"Some Toyota Priuses are still operating on their first set of brake pads after more than 100,000 miles of use, whereas you'd normally assume pads would be replaced after about 30,000 miles," writes Brennan.

Electric cars will still need servicing. What fluids they do use dry out. Batteries and brakes need maintenance, and tires wear out, get punctures and need to be rotated regularly.

Jiffy Lube, for example, lists thirty-four services offered beyond the oil change, including filter replacement, exterior and glass cleaning, shock-absorber maintenance, vehicle alignment, wiper replacement and preparing a vehicle for its annual inspection. EVAdoption notes, however, that fourteen of these services — or 41% — will no longer be needed when EVs come to dominate the market. Another six services (18%) will be of low to medium importance.

In response, in 2021 Jiffy Lube began rolling out its "Electric Vehicle Signature Service," which includes a multipoint safety inspection, tire rotation, brake care and more. Jiffy Lube, owned by Shell Oil, is even experimenting with placing electric charging stations at its facilities as a means of topping off the vehicle while it's already in the service bay.

The new EV package is being trialed at several locations in California, Oregon, Texas and Florida.

"The EV driver and owner is a challenge," Edward Hymes, president of Jiffy Lube, told *Forbes* contributor Dale Buss. "It's important that we get Jiffy Lube seen as a viable and credible solution in EV maintenance. Regardless of when drivers shift to EVs, we need to be ready."

Dennis Clark, formerly of Honda Innovations, throws a bit of caution into the mix.

Although the general consensus is that electric vehicles will need less service, "we don't have enough vehicles on the road to know that for sure yet," he told me.

Automotive industry consultant Glenn Mercer is also on the fence.

"Electric vehicles won't require repairs?" he ponders. "The same doomsaying was made in the 1990s when warranty work made some dealers say they won't have anything to repair."

That clearly wasn't the case then, and it isn't the case now.

In addition to the threat to service revenue, EVs will mean fewer aftermarket parts purchases. McKinsey predicts that electric car owners will spend 40% less on aftermarket parts than do owners of internal combustion engine vehicles.

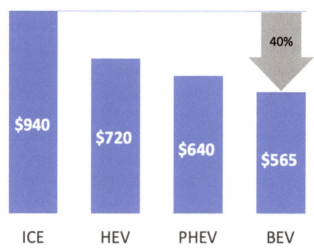

To be sure, Jiffy Lube may be in a more precarious business than dealers — after all, their whole business is centered on the lube and oil change — but diversifying service options is a key lesson for any operation organized around vehicle maintenance and repair.

SENSORS, SENSORS EVERYWHERE

Modern cars, as I've pointed out in previous chapters, are more like computers on wheels than were their purely mechanical ancestors. This should bode well for franchise dealerships, which will be best equipped to service these increasingly complex vehicles.

Let's look at just one component: the windshield.

It's easy to think of the windshield as simply a way to keep the outside away from the inside of our car — hardly a high-tech job. And indeed, for most of automotive history, windshield repair was not particularly different than replacing the glass in any other window frame.

Windshields today are not just glass, though — they have built-in sensors and cameras that require precise diagnostics, calibration and alignment. If your proximity detection sensor is out of whack, you could wind up slamming into the car in front of you. Even a minuscule difference during the replacement process can affect the performance of these systems.

That's why BMW requests that special "electromagnetic compatibility screws" be used in repairs — so that they do not interfere with advanced driver-assistance systems (ADAS). Incorrect glass could distort or block the heads-up displays that project onto the windshield glass and are appearing in more and more BMW models these days.

Ford has warned that using aftermarket glass will result in a noisier ride. Ford's official "OEM glass" includes acoustic dampening technology to deliver a quieter experience.

It's not just a comfort issue, but also a functional one — too much wind or other background noise can interfere with the functioning of the vehicle's voice-activated controls.

Other manufacturers are demanding (or at least strongly suggesting) that replacement windshields use only OEM glass rather than some less expensive aftermarket alternative.

This will only get more critical when autonomous vehicles become widespread and rely exclusively on sensors rather than human senses.

Windshields are now integrated with such ADAS features as blind-spot monitoring, lane-departure warning, lane-keep assist and adaptive cruise control, which maintains a fixed distance between your car and the one in front of you by automatically adjusting your acceleration. Even a one-degree change in a sensor's orientation can put you at risk.

"There will be a big fight for the repair of these more lucrative parts, like glass. We're starting to see it already," Repairify president Tony Rimas told me. "If dealers are the only people to get those types of parts

CHAPTER EIGHT   163

or materials, it could be a real windfall. On the other hand, if fleets dominate in the future and can do their own service, dealers may lose out."

The industry is moving fast, but insurance companies are still "behind the curve," says Aaron Schulenburg, executive director of the Society of Collision Repair Specialists.

The typical insurance company is expecting a $500 bill for a new windshield. The price for the latest smart windshields can be four to five times that amount.

The price of a new Tesla Model S windshield, for example, is $1,049. For a Porsche 911, it's $2,110.

Gorilla Glass is another issue. It's a tougher and thinner material that's favored in everything from iPhones to car windshields, but it can run twice the price of even the more expensive "OEM glass" windshield.

NOT JUST WINDSHIELDS

As autonomous functionality becomes more commonplace, sensors not just in the windshield, but also elsewhere on the car will need regular calibration. Most autonomous vehicles use lidar pulsed laser sensors to navigate. If these get jolted out of alignment — whether due to an accident, poor weather or just general wear and tear — the car will not run properly. And while some sensors can calibrate themselves, even the best will require physical alignment at some point.

Will regulations someday require "proof of calibration" to operate an autonomous vehicle, much like cars need to go in for a smog test periodically? What will be the penalty for an uncalibrated lidar unit?

Sensors fall into four main categories:

1. Front-facing camera sensors. These are used for everything from emergency braking to automatic high-beam activation and dimming. Some vehicles also have a 360-degree "around-view" camera system, with small cameras on the front, rear and sides of the vehicle.

2. Front-facing radar sensors. These are used for adaptive cruise control, forward collision warning and automatic emergency braking. They are usually mounted in the front of the car, but some rear-collision warning and blind-spot monitoring systems use small radar sensors mounted under the sideview mirrors, behind the rear bumper or even in the taillights. Lidar fits into this category.
3. Ultrasonic sensors. These are used for parking assist and self-parking systems. They're installed in the front and rear bumper covers, where they use reflected high-frequency sound waves to detect people, cars and other objects in close proximity.
4. Steering-angle sensors. These are used for lane-departure warning, lane keeping and adaptive headlight control. They are usually built into the steering column to measure the degree of wheel rotation.

Companies such as Autel are trying to capitalize on the coming calibration revolution, selling a calibration system for dealers.

Others, like Zoox (acquired by Amazon in 2020), are developing tools to calibrate their own autonomous vehicles — and will eventually make those tools available for fleet customers.

Repairify's asTech provides remote diagnostic services and products to dealers and others in the collision industry and has been actively acquiring sensor calibration companies.

"Today a lot of the systems in a car are separate and don't talk to each other," Rimas notes. "The front-end camera does one thing, the front-end sensor does something else. We're trying to bring a lot of the electronic components together in one centralized system. A system where all the pieces talk to each other will speed up the industry. Remember how when the iPhone first came out, you had to be on Wi-Fi to update apps? With today's smartphones, you don't even notice apps updating on their own. The exact same thing will happen with cars."

Lidar is not new. It was created in the 1970s by NASA to develop spacecraft. In the 1990s, it helped with topographic mapping of Earth's

CHAPTER EIGHT   165

surface. Lidar helps governments plan roads and it helps surveyors and construction companies pick the best places to put buildings, especially if there's uneven terrain.

But a rocket here or a building there doesn't compare with the hundreds of millions of vehicles hurtling down the road at dangerous speeds. A misaligned sensor in a car equipped with ADAS could cause unnecessary emergency braking, double vision when looking through the windshield or (in a less high-speed concern) poor self-parking performance.

A BRIGHT SIDE?

There's a bright side lurking behind all the change: The transition to higher-tech windshields, ADAS components and all manner of automotive-adapted gizmos constitutes a significant opportunity for dealers who can act quickly.

How so?

The smarter cars get, the more drivers will insist on taking their vehicle to a repair shop that knows what it's doing. Who has the state-of-the-art equipment required? Who has the most skilled technicians or the time and systems in place to ensure everything is fully functional and safe?

Is that going to be "Eddie's Garage" or the dealer where you bought your car?

"It used to be that a dealer had a body shop for one reason: to fix the car just well enough so the customer will buy another," Rimas told me. "The proliferation of electronic components plays well for body shops. Some are making 12% net to sales, while the main dealership is lucky to be making 5%. In the next five years, unless these guys shift to a service-first franchise model, it won't matter if they sell another car."

The tight relationship between OEM and dealer works to the dealer's advantage in this case. "Manufacturers won't refer you to a Jiffy Lube" for a technically complex repair, notes Holman Strategic Ventures' Bill Cariss. "That's billions of dollars of service. Dealers will love this!"

"Whoever figures out how to be the 'CarMax of Repair' will be a big winner," adds FM Capital partner Chase Fraser. "This will most likely be a dealer with two hundred service bays and a cool waiting room."

Andrew Gordon, the former CEO of DealerScience, sees two types of facilities emerging: the big dealers (Fraser's "CarMax of Repair") and smaller, more specialized shops.

"It's like how you don't take your MacBook to an Apple Store for repairs unless it's still under warranty," Gordon told me. "You find a local, cheaper fix-it shop. You don't need a $25 million facility for that."

How often will you need to take your ADAS-capable car in for something like sensor calibration? Once a month? Once a year?

In that way, a car is very different than a computer, Gordon adds, where major repairs are rare and operating system updates "don't require a trip to Apple for every update."

Fortunately, the computerization of the car, coupled with wireless connectivity, means your car will know in real time when a problem is brewing before you do — and it can communicate any issues directly to the OEM, which can then suggest a repair, timetable and the most appropriate dealer or repair shop, all without the vehicle's owner needing to know or make a decision.

Got a warranty? Or did you get a message that your vehicle needs a recall repair? Then you're definitely taking your car into the dealer.

But how does the dealer get paid? OEMs bake into the price of a new car a credit to the dealer for warranty or recall work. Essentially, you are prepaying for that warranty work when you buy a car. The dealer submits an invoice to the OEM for the work.

Dealers will need to devise new ways to engender customer loyalty. That will require innovative thinking, superlative service and, most of all, figuring out ways to get the consumer onto the dealer's lot at a time when, with driveway delivery and online purchasing on the rise, those in-person touchpoints are fewer and farther between than ever before.

RECALL WORK

In 2021, GM was forced to recall more than 140,000 Chevy Bolt electric vehicles due to the risk that their batteries might spontaneously catch fire while parked. GM has confirmed thirteen such fires globally. These EV fires don't appear to be more severe than similar fires in gas-powered cars, but they last longer, resulting in more damage to the vehicle.

Car aficionado and collector Jay Leno commented in an interview with CNBC's Shepard Smith that, "The advantage, if there is one, to an EV fire is, it doesn't blow up. You're in it, you smell something, there's smoke, and then it doesn't go up in a ball, the way a gasoline car would."

The GM recalls followed a similar recall of electric vehicles manufactured by Hyundai, which uses the same battery from Seoul-based LG Chem. (Shares of the battery maker were down 11% following the recall news.) The recall cost Hyundai nearly $1 billion; for GM, it was close to double that. In October 2021, LG agreed to reimburse GM for $1.9 billion in costs and expenses associated with the Bolt recall.

Some analysts worry that the costs of such an expensive recall will be passed on to consumers as higher prices and may lead to a temporary shortage of new vehicles (or new batteries) from affected OEMs. The four leading electric battery makers — LG, Panasonic, Samsung and CATL — are all located in Asia and are running at close to full capacity.

All cars — electric and otherwise — suffer from recalls. But for ICE vehicles, the recalls usually involve faulty components such as airbags, ignition switches and floormats — all relatively inexpensive to replace.

Not so with EVs. Batteries account for about 40% of the total price of the vehicle.

Recalls are the bane of the automotive industry. They cost the OEMs billions of dollars and often require loaner vehicles to be provided for potentially extended periods of time.

But they are also an opening for dealers facing declining service work. And, as Jade Terreberry, director of dealer sales analytics at

Kelley Blue Book notes, as modern vehicles get more complicated, "we expect to see an increase in recalls."

In 2020, there were twenty-nine million automotive recalls mandated by the U.S. National Highway Traffic Safety Administration and more than eighty-three million voluntary recalls. That translates into more than one in every four vehicles on American roads with at least one open recall.

Beyond the recall itself, "Car dealers can hit a double when a vehicle is in for recall work," writes Steve Finlay for WardsAuto. That's because OEMs, first of all, must pay the dealership to repair the problem that prompted the recall.

But second, while the vehicle is in the shop for that work, technicians may detect other problems, which they'll be happy to work on if the customer approves. (Such upselling should be for legitimate reasons, of course, not merely to pad the bill, Finlay cautions.)

No one wants a recall. But dealers, who can count on a guaranteed payment per vehicle repair from the OEM, can turn these lemons into retail lemonade.

In the meantime, GM is advising Bolt owners — "out of an abundance of caution" — to avoid depleting their battery below approximately 70 miles of remaining range, refrain from parking their vehicles inside and avoid charging them unattended overnight.

WHERE YA GONNA CHARGE?

Dealerships looking to add new revenue-generating services should consider adding charge spots to their properties to entice EV drivers to make regular visits. This could be part of the overall service, as Jiffy Lube is exploring, or a standalone offering for EV owners who cannot charge at home (apartment dwellers with no dedicated parking spot, for example).

Audi is doing exactly that with a "quick-charging hub" that opened in December 2021 at the Nuremberg Exhibition Center.

Why would a dealer want to get into the charge-spot business?

CHAPTER EIGHT 169

Any reason to get customers into the dealership is another chance to sell. That might be accessories the customer didn't choose when making the initial purchase. It might be an entirely new car if the customer's existing vehicle is getting old or if its lease period is running out.

Any technique to increase engagement at a time when customers don't need to visit a dealer as frequently should be welcomed.

What can dealers do to bring customers in for a charge?

Free coffee or donuts is always an enticement. (Although these days, your morning bagel and latte are often delivered to you.)

A discount on charging fees could help too.

How about a free car wash while you're there? (And would you like to install a roof rack while you're at it?)

Dealers could also provide the customer with a battery health report or certify that their ADAS sensors are clean and aligned.

Indeed, the opportunity to upsell customers is the key reason why dealers may want to offer free or discounted services. Customers may spend most of their time checking Facebook while they're waiting, but there are all kinds of goodies to offer: new steering wheel covers, winter wheels and tires, tinted windows, brake rotors, undercoating and rust proofing, bike racks, all-weather floormats, paint protection, vehicle-tracking devices, even branded keychains.

David Stringer, CEO of the Insignia Group, says that small to average-sized dealerships should generate about $250,000 in revenue a year from accessory sales. Larger dealerships can generate millions of dollars in revenue. The overall accessory sales market is worth about $46 billion per year.

"The cars we own are an extension of our personality, and vehicle customization is a great way to express our individuality," Stringer says. "For dealerships looking to thrive in these challenging times, accessory sales are a great way to bolster revenue and uncover hidden profits."

Education will be key here.

"Most consumers don't know the breadth or depth of the accessories dealerships offer and, as a result, often turn to aftermarket companies to purchase the add-ons they want," he says.

Other upsells are less tangible: The opportunity to refinance your car loan or reappraise your insurance policy are valuable to both dealer and customer.

Why would an EV owner want to charge at a dealership rather than at a public charge spot? It depends on where the dealership is located. Many dealerships are located on or near highways, which makes for a convenient stop on the way to work.

Today, charging is mostly first come, first served, which leads to problems when all the charge spots are full. In the future, "reservations" for specific times, organized by the vehicle's (or the dealer's) app could resolve some of these timing concerns. (As I noted previously, autonomous vehicles could be programmed to visit the dealer for a charge at 2 a.m.)

The more useful the app is, the more loyalty the EV owner will have to the dealer, the OEM (or Starbucks). An app could even provide a daily valuation: How much is your car worth today? How much tomorrow? When is the best time to sell? If you're already at the dealer, you're more likely to take the path of least resistance and buy and sell there if the app so advises.

All the while, the dealer is increasing customer touchpoints, strengthening brand perception and building up a database of current owners that can be leveraged. OEMs that work closely with their dealerships will be able to strengthen the lifetime value of their customers.

Companies such as Seattle-based Recurrent can help. Automotive Ventures made an investment in the company in 2022. The startup's technology measures an electric car battery's health. Dubbed by tech pundits as the "Carfax for batteries," Recurrent's algorithm downloads four data points from registered EVs up to three times a day: charging status, battery level, odometer and the car computer's range estimate.

Recurrent addresses the gradual deterioration of a battery's ability to hold a charge and how that affects the residual value of the car. Moreover, EVs using Recurrent's software will be able to command a

CHAPTER EIGHT   171

premium compared to non-Recurrent EVs, CEO Scott Case wrote on the company's blog.

BATTERY SWAP FOR FUN AND PROFIT

While charging is a recurring event, at some point in their lifespan, electric vehicles will need a new battery.

Could dealers be the destination for battery swapping?

NIO already offers a battery swap service in China and has completed over a million exchanges. That type of business hasn't caught on in the West, but a more limited form of battery swap could still take hold.

In mid-2021, California-based battery swapping company Ample raised $160 million from investors including Shell Ventures for its modular, lightweight battery swap architecture. Ample stresses that "carmakers don't need to redesign their cars to work with Ample technology" and that "a whole city can be deployed in weeks." Ample could be the backbone for a dealer-operated swapping option.

Here's an example: You've bought an electric vehicle with a modest 200-mile range; now, you want to go on a 500-mile road trip to Disneyland. Could a dealer swap out your smaller battery for one that can go the distance when you need it, then return your original battery upon your return?

At some point (soon, we all hope), charging times will drop from their current forty minutes to five minutes or fewer. Does that obviate the need for a free blueberry muffin?

Not necessarily.

EVs will still need a charge, even if it goes faster. Faster charges may limit physical interaction, but experienced dealers know how much upselling can be accomplished in just five minutes!

TIRED OF CHANGING TIRES

Electric vehicles wear out tires at a much faster rate than do internal combustion engine cars. The reasoning is simple: The vehicles, with their plethora of lithium-ion batteries, are rather heavy, and the near-instant torque stresses the tires.

"You don't need to hunt for long to find a Tesla owner who's replaced their tires after a mere 10,000 miles," Brennan notes.

On-demand tire replacement company Zohr (one of Brennan's investments) says its EV customers come back for tire replacements 30% more frequently than do internal combustion engine drivers.

Scott Clark, an executive vice president at Michelin, estimates that conventional tires on an electric vehicle probably wear out 20% faster.

Tire manufacturers such as Michelin have, in response, developed "low-rolling resistance" tires that reduce the amount of energy that's lost when starting a "cold tire" from a standing start.

That's important, says Michelin North America chairman and president Alexis Garcin, since "20% to 30% of the fuel consumption of the car is directly impacted by the tire."

Michelin's new tire design should translate into greater battery range for EVs, although there's a trade-off that not everyone will love: less grip and poorer overall handling.

ExxonMobil estimates that improving tire pressure could increase an EV's range by up to 7% without needing a larger or redesigned battery. (Forty-eight percent of tires suffer from "significant air loss" over time simply from normal use.)

Exxon teamed up with the Geely Research Institute and Shandong Linglong Tyre Company in China to analyze the relationship between tires and EV efficiency. Among the findings: Upgrading tires to the latest technology across all Chinese electric vehicles could save 90 gigawatt-hours per year, enough to power fifty thousand Chinese households.

The upshot of the EV-tire conundrum is a confusing dichotomy: Tires represent an opportunity for dealers to earn extra service revenue at a time when other parts divisions are hurting, while at the same time, new tire technology could make tires more efficient — even with electric cars — counteracting that potential silver lining.

One way to find further cost-efficiency is by automating the process. That's something automotive startup RoboTire is working on. Using robotics and artificial intelligence, the Plymouth, Michigan-based company aims to "free your hard-to-find, highly trained technicians to spend less time on tire changes and more on higher-margin service and repairs."

If wait times drop, "loyal customers increase," the company emphasizes.

(Full disclosure: I'm an investor in RoboTire.)

"Tires-as-a-service" is another way to spin this opportunity: Would consumers pay a monthly subscription fee that covered new tires and repairs?

Modern Tire Dealer magazine surveyed tire executives about their recommendations for dealers. Here is a sampling of replies:

- Dale Harrigle, chief engineer for product development, consumer replacement at Bridgestone Americas: "I think the primary focus [for dealers] should be on wear and rolling resistance. When they find a tire that works well on EVs, it would be good to stay with that tire."
- Mauricio Mendez Sotelo, technical product management, research and development, passenger and light truck tires at Continental Tire the Americas: Checking air pressure "will be much more critical for EVs in terms of the contribution of the pressure of the tire to the weight of the car. Pay attention to inflation pressure."
- Rodrigo Uso, senior technical account manager and technical sales team leader North America at Hankook Tire America: "In order to make sure the end user continues to experience the same performance of their vehicle, it's extremely important that dealers know how to convince their customers to use only the

OEM tire because it is the right fit."

- Richard Smallwood, CEO and president of Sumitomo Rubber North America: "Not every EV customer will have the same wants and desires. One size does not fit all, so the dealer needs to listen to the customer and then know which tire options are available to them."

DRIVEWAY OR STORE?

As businesses such as Carvana and Lithia push to make driveway delivery a norm, service and repairs will conveniently shift away from the dealership's shop to the customer's home or office.

"Routine service at a customer's place of business or home is a huge opportunity to grow revenue," AutoProfit's Ed French told me.

In its simplest form, this could mean the dealer picks up your car and returns it later in the day, rather than requiring you to go out of your way to drive it in, then secure a loaner car for the day or week.

I recently invested in a company called HopDrive, which offers dealers exactly this service. The company notes that 80% of customers would switch to a dealership that offers pickup and delivery, and that 50% of customers would pay $20 for such a concierge service.

I can also envision a scenario where a vehicle and mechanic come to your driveway and conduct repairs on the spot. That's what NuBrakes does; it's another company in which I've invested. They deliver the convenience of trusted repairs without your having to take your car into the shop.

It doesn't have to be in your driveway.

If your vehicle knows you spend an hour at Costa Coffee every Thursday morning, it can send someone to rotate your tires or replace your coolant right there, before you're even done with your pumpkin spice latte.

The Chinese EV maker NIO did something similar with battery swapping originally, sending a switch truck to your office. The company now is focused on manufacturing easy-to-move pop-up swapping stations, like those from Ample, which are, in any case, much more scalable.

FixMyCar is a Michigan-based startup that sends certified mechanics to your home or office. They offer extended business hours and weekend availability. The service is currently available in Detroit, Dallas, Houston and Austin, with plans to expand nationwide.

FixMyCar can replace batteries, starters and spark plugs; do light engine and brake repairs; and run routine maintenance (such as oil changes for nonelectric vehicles).

These mobile mechanic services cost 20% to 30% less than at dealerships and independent repair shops.

"This changes the way people think about car repair and empowers them to take control of their vehicle's health," says FixMyCar founder Prashant Salla.

In the face of competition from startups, dealers must consider offering driveway repairs as well, whether simply to stay competitive or as a premium service.

"I can't imagine a world where you'd want to go into a dealership for service if someone is willing to pick your car up, even if it costs $25 more," FUSE Autotech's Andrew Walser told me. "Is my time worth more than $25 to drop off and pick up a car?"

CAR WASH AS A PROFIT CENTER

"A tunnel car wash can generate $2 million a year with 40% margins and 20% EBITDA," points out consultant Glenn Mercer. "A well-run car wash can reach breakeven within the first five days of the month. And their usefulness is growing as states move to forbid curbside car washes with suds going into the gutter."

Most dealers didn't get into the business to wash cars — even though many dealers have a small car wash on their premises to keep the cars they're selling shiny and clean — but confronted with decreasing service revenue and increased margin compression, any new source of revenue is welcome.

Car washes could be offered as a subscription — the customer pays $20 a month and gets unlimited cleaning. That turns the lowly car wash into a recurring revenue stream, especially if, like a gym membership, drivers don't fully take advantage of their subscription terms. If I'm a dealer, why not try it?

Other business models include providing customers a "car wash code" when they're ready to pay for their repairs, and "no limit" free washes for life, provided you bought your car at that dealership.

Car washes result in happier customers.

"There is a large increase in CSI [customer satisfaction index] scores when people get their car back clean," says Harry Schleeter, president of Broadway Equipment Company, a manufacturer of car wash systems. "Today's dealership business is all about improving or having a great customer experience."

Car washes could be a profit center of their own, writes Jack Allison for CarWash.com. Allison, president of Engineered Car Wash Systems of Birmingham, Alabama, envisions three types of car wash services:

- Free car washes during a service visit for existing customers.
- Discount washes to customers even if not combined with a service visit.
- Full-price washes to the general public, leading to even more profits.

The latter, Allison suggests, "may even lead to a car wash customer coming into the showroom to purchase a new vehicle."

Car washes come in two flavors: hand-wash and automatic. To scale, automatic is the way to go.

"When the volume of daily washes is so large that the hand-wash operation can't keep up or when the volume is so large that labor costs are more than the monthly equipment payment, it's time to consider the purchase of an automatic car wash system," writes Bud Abraham for *Dealer Ops*.

CHAPTER EIGHT   177

Automated car washes also mean you don't have to have a dedicated staff member waiting around for the next car to clean by hand — or to dry by hand, which can easily eat up ten minutes of valuable service time, especially if an autonomous car comes in for its cleaning in the wee hours of the morning.

Car washes, a low-tech, high-revenue option, could be a template for other dealer-offered services, such as cosmetic repairs.

"Dealers should be thinking about setting up cosmetic repair departments," Tony Rimas told me. "Painting bumpers is one more way to diversify revenue," as are dent popping and wheel refurbishment.

And once the paint job is done and the dents are smoothed out, you're going to need that car wash.

COLLISION SHOP OPPORTUNITY

Today's vehicles have many more sensors, cameras, radar, lidar and complex material construction than ever before. Increased vehicle complexity means more frequent need for calibration of key components and increased repair difficulty.

Many of the most popular vehicles in the U.S. weigh more than 8,500 pounds as consumer tastes move toward pickups and SUVs. More heavy vehicles on the roads equates to greater severity of accidents.

According to automotive consulting firm CCC's "Crash Course" report, the average appraisal on a vehicle in need of repair rose by 5.5% to $3,421 in 2020. The report cites "consumer preference for light trucks and vehicles loaded up with the newest technology" as one of the main causes for more complex and expensive repairs.

The CCC report notes further that electronic repair components are starting to make up a larger portion of total repair estimates, showing an increase from 4% to 6% in the past year. The two most common components were cameras and sensors, which cost an average of $110 and $577, respectively, to replace.

Even in minor collisions, ADAS equipment can require a full recalibration. According to the report, about 5% of vehicles repaired in the past year included a calibration entry, the average price of which was just below $260.

The increasing complexity of vehicles affords dealers with their own collision repair shops the opportunity to provide consumers with peace of mind based on the correct tools, technicians and training to ensure their vehicle is returned to its pre-accident condition.

According to the latest research from the National Automobile Dealers Association (NADA), the percentage of dealerships operating on-site body shops decreased in 2021 to 35.7%, down from 37.3% in 2020. There were approximately 5,953 dealers operating body shops in 2021.

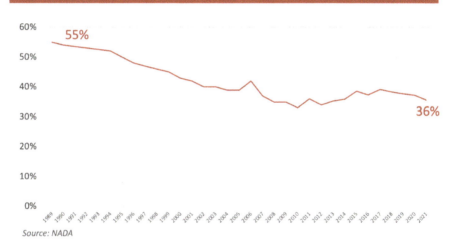

AUTONOMY AND THE MODERN DEALER

Autonomous vehicles won't need a driver to get to a dealer for service; they will simply drive themselves. And what better time to do that than in the middle of the night when the car would (usually) be sitting idle in a driveway?

The same is true, by the way, for electric cars searching for a charge spot when there's none at home. They can navigate to a preferred charging location and, since the vehicle won't be experiencing downtime at 3 a.m., it can go wherever the price is right, regardless of how far away it is (within reason). Waiting in line for service becomes a piece of cake when you, the driver, can remain snug in bed.

Moreover, do you really care where your self-driving car was serviced or charged if you don't need to be present when that happens? Not really. It could be a franchise dealer's lot or an independent repair shop with dozens of technicians. Just send over the invoice and hope that your car "chose" the cheapest, most professional place.

The image of thousands of AVs heading out at midnight to be charged or repaired is spooky, to be sure. Moreover, it will entail significant changes at the dealer — most important, a requirement for staff (human or robotic) to work 24/7.

There's one other possibility we haven't considered yet, and it's a contrarian one: that autonomous vehicles will actually *increase* service work by dealers. The argument, which Dr. Lance Eliot, artificial intelligence expert and chief AI scientist at Techbrium, lays out in *Forbes,* goes something like this:

Many (if not most) autonomous vehicles will be shared as part of fleets. That means they'll be in use far more frequently than cars owned by an individual, which as we've noted, don't get driven more than 5% to 10% of the time.

All those extra miles result in more wear and tear and, as a result, more maintenance work. It may not be broken-down cars or accident repair, but regular alignment and calibration of sensors and cameras will become critical when the cars — like the dealer service staff — are operating 24/7.

And with so much computerization in the car these days, well, anyone who's ever used a PC (I'm going to go out on a limb and say that's all of us at this point) knows that there are plenty of unexpected glitches and hiccups. It's not going to magically work all the time.

"Wear and tear is a law of physics," writes Eliot. "No matter how good the artificial intelligence might be on an autonomous car, it's still a car. More miles translate into more wear and tear. Parts are going to need to be replaced. Ongoing maintenance is going to be keenly desired, especially since the lost revenue from any downtime is going to be hurtful."

Wear and tear on the *inside* of a car will also become a factor for shared autonomous vehicles.

"Think of all those people, getting into and out of their driverless cars, hour after hour, all day long, all week long," writes Eliot. "I doubt these passengers will be mindful of their milkshakes that spill."

Unfortunately (for dealers), cleaning the inside of a vehicle can't be automated in the same way as running it through an exterior tunnel car wash. Removing leftover french fries requires vacuum cleaners and human beings to crawl into the back seat (although by the time autonomous vehicles truly come of age, we may delegate that task to robots).

Will the future of automotive retail lead to more or less service? Dealers need to be prepared for all eventualities and to think outside the box about new revenue opportunities to replace the good old days of the familiar internal combustion engine, with its more regular service intervals and greater number of moving parts.

CHAPTER NINE

THE FUTURE OF THE DEALERSHIP

"The future is already here. It's just not very evenly distributed."
— **William Gibson, Award-Winning Speculative Fiction Writer**

Tim Kelly's family had owned Kelly Subaru in Chattanooga, Tennessee, for forty-nine years. Subaru is a brand that engenders passionate loyalty, but as Kelly quipped in an email he sent to me in early 2021, "We're at 'peak Subaru,'" explaining why he was selling his dealership now, even as it's having a tough time keeping up with the sales volume.

Kelly Subaru has been a cash cow. It generated over $36 million in state and local sales taxes in 2020 alone. And yet, "This is the highest valuation for the dealership we're ever going to get," Kelly explained to me.

Crown Automotive Group is the new owner of Kelly Subaru, and Tim Kelly has a new job: He's mayor of Chattanooga.

Like Kelly, former DealerScience CEO Andrew Gordon facilitated the sale of his family's Boston-area Honda dealership in 2017. Gordon's grandfather started the business, and then his father ran it for forty years. The youngest Gordon was slated to take over.

For Gordon, it wasn't the price that was key, but rather the writing he saw on the wall.

"We saw a shift toward more digital retailers and more competitors trying to sell things online," he told me. "We saw that our big defensible piece against online sales was dealer franchise laws. But those are only strong if cars are not sold online. Once that happens, and they can be delivered from one big hub close to the city center to an entire region, that would be a real threat to dealers."

The dealership was sold to Victory Automotive Group.

Then there's Tony Rimas. Before he was president of Dallas-based Repairify, Rimas headed up operations for the Red McCombs Automotive Group.

"We originally had four Hyundai stores in San Antonio," Rimas told me. "We created one mega Hyundai store, with the others serving as feeders. Now we sell more Hyundais than ever."

These stories underscore how dealers are currently in a precarious position. With the pace of change accelerating, and with all the uncertainty around the future of the automotive retail landscape, many dealers are taking the opportunity to sell their stores.

Pre-COVID-19, dealerships were already suffering from a steady deterioration of net profit margins, which according to NADA (the National Automotive Dealers Association) had dropped from a 2.8% net profit share of sales in 2014 to 2.1% in 2020.

Such a decline may not sound like a lot, but if the trend continues post-COVID-19, it will make running a dealership an increasingly challenging proposition.

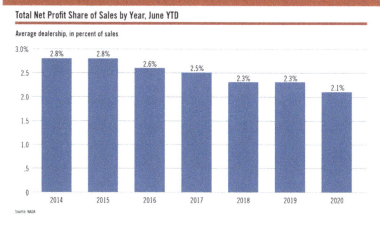

The increased pace of sales of dealerships is being driven by factors including sky-high valuations, COVID-19 and microchip-induced inventory shortages driving record profitability, and voracious public dealer groups with inflated market caps looking to acquire other dealerships.

Throughout this book, we've explored the impact of many factors bearing down on automotive retailing — questions of convenience, ownership, connectivity, autonomy, power source, vehicle production and service. We've investigated what these themes mean for consumers, OEMs and dealers.

In this final chapter, I want to get prescriptive and provide specific recommendations. For example:

- What can dealers do to stay relevant in a rapidly changing retail environment?
- What's driving the blurring of lines between retail and wholesale?
- How can dealers address relentless margin compression?
- What are the implications if (when) big tech players, such as Amazon, get in the game?
- When is the right time to sell your dealership?

GOOD TIME FOR A CHANGE

"The best time to change is when you're making a lot of money," Gordon told me. "Not when you're about to go under."

Or, as John F. Kennedy famously said, "The time to repair the roof is when the sun is shining."

That time is increasingly looking like "now" as the pace of technological change accelerates, threatening to further disrupt the business.

Dealers and OEMs have succeeded thus far despite themselves. Many still rely on manual processes, pushing paper around and otherwise using old, clunky systems and software products that don't talk to one another.

But entrepreneurs look at automotive, and they say, "Wow, it's an ample space with money being spent, but it presents inefficiencies. Let's innovate and solve this."

One of the biggest problems for dealerships is that "the business is very day-to-day," notes former Honda Innovations' Dennis Clark. "Dealers don't have time to think about the future."

But by being a slave to the month-to-month sales cycle, many dealers never have the opportunity to lift up their heads and get perspective on some of the larger themes evolving that will affect them.

"They don't have the luxury to look out further and anticipate change," Clark continues. They get the cars the OEMs want them to take; they build the showroom experiences OEMs have asked them to create; they only have freedom to choose from a limited number of third-party vendors. "They don't have a lot of ability to innovate."

To be sure, dealers will continue to be profitable for the next five years, but storm clouds are gathering on the horizon and heading this way (although it's hard to quantify exactly when they'll hit and what will be their magnitude). When these threats start to impact dealerships' revenues and bottom lines, that's when the valuation multiples of physical dealerships may start to collapse.

It's hard to see what's coming when you're in the middle of the good times.

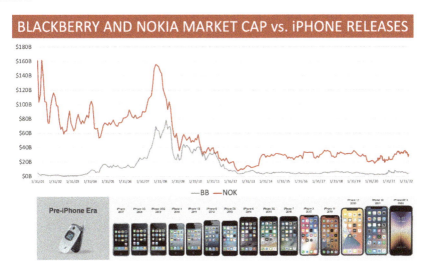

"The year the iPhone came out, sales at Nokia were at an all-time high," recalls Clark. "A few years later, the market was very different. No one wanted a Nokia phone. Or a BlackBerry either."

Dealers who can envision a future five or ten years down the road realize that, while they may be at the top of their game today, the time may soon arrive when it's prudent to get out while the going is still good. In another five years, the Tim Kellys of the world might not get the same prices offered in 2022 or 2023.

For family-owned businesses like Kelly's or Gordon's, it's even more critical: If you sell now, can you help preserve your family's wealth?

In 2008, I was working for Cox Enterprises which, in addition to Cox Automotive and Autotrader, owned several traditional media properties. Prior to the internet, owning newspapers and radio stations proved to be a very defensible and profitable business, with newspapers trading at fifteen times earnings.

But as the internet gained traction, consumer eyeballs migrated online and valuations came crashing down. For example, in a dramatic fall from grace, the *New York Daily News* sold for $1 in cash plus the assumptions of pension obligations.

 CHAPTER NINE   **187**

The same could very well happen to dealerships. What can we learn from previous disruptions?

That's what this chapter will attempt to outline.

TRUST

A few years ago, I was visiting Longo Toyota, the largest dealership (by volume) in the world. From a fifty-acre footprint of land near West Covina in Southern California (made famous as the setting for the TV series *Crazy Ex-Girlfriend),* Longo sells between twenty-five thousand and thirty thousand vehicles consistently, year after year.

At the end of my tour of the facilities, I was waiting out front to pick up my car and started a conversation with a gentleman who was in for regular vehicle service. It turns out that he had driven north from San Diego that morning, a two-and-a-half-hour drive, for an oil change. When I quizzed the guy about why he would do such a thing, he responded, "I have been buying cars from Longo Toyota for the past twenty-five years and have purchased my last five cars from them. I would never even think about taking my car anywhere else for service!"

In the previous chapter, we looked at some of the services dealers could offer to keep customers loyal: electric charge spots, overnight car washes, sensor calibration. All of these are meant to keep customers coming back.

But, beyond these short-term tactics, what really keeps consumers engaged with dealerships is something less tangible: trust.

Trust begets loyalty, and loyalty begets lifetime value of a customer.

In the future, it's going to be more important than ever for dealers to engender loyalty and hold on to their customers.

Consumers can't necessarily discern from a website a dealer's trustworthiness. That's why there's nothing like an in-person visit to help demonstrate a dealership's credibility, although even this is under pressure with the shift to more online and remote services.

A dealer's reputation can go a long way to calm worries. After all, customers don't care which merchant they buy from on Amazon as long as the seller has five stars and offers next-day delivery.

After the purchase of a home, a vehicle is the largest, most considered purchase most of us will ever make. It's a multifaceted, complex transaction. So building trust, whether online or off, will require significant work. And changes will need to be made to counteract longstanding suspicions around dealer trust.

A 2018 Gallup poll indicated that, in terms of Americans' most and least trusted professions, car salespeople were second to last on the list, just barely above politicians!

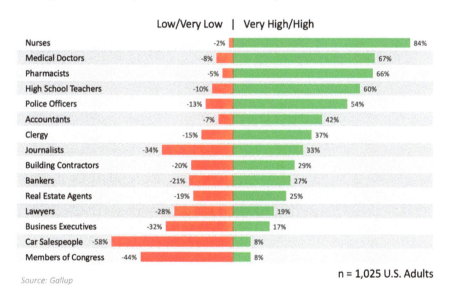

"Consumers don't trust us, and I hate that," Honda of Seattle COO Babak Mohammadi admits. "We've got to change the industry. We've got to show there's a better way."

Mohammadi's dealership adopted strategies to enhance trust. It decoupled sales commissions from the profitability of a sale, eliminated the handoff between a salesperson and the F&I department and adopted no-haggle pricing and transparent financing information.

This is where the internet can help.

"Consumers simply don't trust that they are paying an appropriate price," notes Brian Hafer, VP of marketing for AutoMD. "Their view of the whole experience is, generally, not a positive one." Hafer was speaking about service and repair shops, although his advice is relevant across the dealer value proposition.

"But there is good news," he stresses. "Consumers are going online to check price quotes and reviews and are craving apples-to-apples actual job quotes [for repairs]. So, for shops that are pricing fairly, offering real quotes and keeping up a good digital presence, there is a real chance to improve perception and, with it, their business."

A lot of trust-building can be accomplished online. This includes:

- A well-designed website that addresses customers' needs for vehicle selection, search functionality and transparent pricing.
- Fast response regardless of how the customer contacted the dealer (email, web form, SMS, phone).
- Synchronized "omnichannel" interfaces so that customers who start the process online don't need to begin again from scratch when arriving at the dealership.

Dealership consulting group DrivingSales conducted a study called "How Trust Impacts Car Sales." Among their findings:

HOW TRUST IMPACTS CAR SALES

1.5%
Expect to be satisfied with their experience at a dealership.

99%
Of automotive shoppers expect the process to be a "hassle."

56%
Of shoppers would buy more frequently if the process wasn't so difficult.

50%
Will walk out of a dealership if the dealer requires a test drive before providing a price.

Source: DrivingSales

FIVE FACTORS THAT DETRACT FROM TRUST

- Negative online reviews
- An unhelpful or unknowledgeable sales manager
- Requesting personal information too soon
- Too much negotiation
- Not being taken seriously

Source: Driving Sales

Price transparency is particularly important when it comes to building trust.

Some time back, TrueCar found that consumers believe dealers make about 20% profit on the sale of a $30,000 car. In reality, it's as low as 2.1%, as we saw in the chart from NADA above.

Ironically, consumers believe that a "fair" profit margin on the sale of a new car should be between 10% and 12% and, if told that dealers theoretically made 0% profit on the transaction, TrueCar survey respondents said they would be willing to voluntarily "tip" the dealer 8% on a sale.

Intriguing? Yes.

Sustainable? Hardly.

NEW DELIVERY MODELS

One of the strongest arguments for visiting a brick-and-mortar showroom is to see what's on the lot and to be able to walk away with a car the same day — instant gratification. But as I noted in Chapter Four, with online ordering, if the car of your choice is not available locally, it can be shipped to you from out of state. (While this option was available before, it became much easier when everything moved online.)

If the future continues to evolve in this direction, is there really justification to have fifteen Toyota stores in Atlanta when a single dealership with a sophisticated website would suffice? Isn't that what Tony Rimas discovered in San Antonio?

The winners may be those with scale efficiencies.

Larger dealer groups (and in some cases automakers) may find it prudent to invest in buying up land for huge yards on the outskirts of major metropolitan areas as a kind of staging ground for cars before moving them onto a dealer's lot (or to a customer's driveway). Owning larger dealerships in the right strategic locations may be the best, if not the only, way to succeed.

Andrew Gordon envisions these staging centers as IKEA-like, with customer-facing departments in addition to wholesale activities.

"There will be fewer of them, but they will be prominently located, outside city centers, potentially even handling multiple brands or having nearby showrooms, like an auto mall. They don't have to be downtown," he told me.

The internet has not only made it easier to source vehicles; it's changed the power dynamic.

In the past, if a dealer said there were only blue Priuses available at such-and-such price, you'd have no way of knowing what else was out there. You had to trust the dealer.

Transparency via the web has flipped the dynamic, to the point where incentives and invoice price (the exact amount the dealer paid for the car) are no longer hidden weapons a dealer can pull out when necessary to wear down a customer who doesn't have access to the same "insider information."

Say what you will about the internet and social media these days, but it is clearly a consumer's best friend.

"Remember how involved it used to be just to buy a computer?" Gordon recalls. "You'd have to talk to a product specialist at Best Buy or CompUSA. Now a lower-level person can handle these sales interactions."

Gordon sees that as a positive.

"It's a natural evolution that allows a less sophisticated, less expensive staff person to be more effective. For dealerships, it helps them more easily source staff and control costs, which should help them in the future with margin compression."

BIG TECH AND AUTOMOTIVE

With the advances of online retailing for both new and used cars, how long will it be until we see some of the big tech players — Amazon, Facebook, Alphabet (Google and Waymo's parent company), Apple and others — make more aggressive plays into the automotive space?

While it sounds like Apple is at least a few years away from its autonomous vehicle (see Chapter Six), with Waymo going live around the same time, Amazon might be best positioned to influence the automotive retail channel in the near term.

Remember that in 2020 Amazon acquired self-driving van startup Zoox for $1.3 billion. The rationale was to develop autonomous driving technology, including vehicles, for the purpose of providing a full-stack (client- and server-side) solution for ride-hailing.

Amazon has been working on its own autonomous vehicle technology as well, including last-mile delivery robots — six-wheeled sidewalk bots designed to carry small packages to customers' homes — and drones that can deliver light packages via the air. Amazon has also invested in autonomous driving startup Aurora and EV manufacturer Rivian, and it has tested self-driving trucks powered by autonomous freight startup Embark.

In terms of selling cars online, Amazon has been dabbling for some time:

- Amazon began testing new car sales in Italy and France in 2018, although the pilot was abandoned in 2020.
- In Spain, Amazon launched a car subscription service in partnership with leasing company ALD Automotive, although that pilot, which started in 2019, also has been shut down.
- Amazon was rumored to be in talks with the U.K. government in 2018 to bypass dealerships and sell cars directly to consumers from Amazon.co.uk. So far, nothing has materialized.
- Amazon Vehicles is the company's research and information subsite, with reviews, new and used car pricing, specs and videos, positioned to creep into car sales.

I believe that Carvana would be a natural acquisition for Amazon. The two are both direct-to-consumer innovators that share a relentless focus on meeting and exceeding shopper expectations. They both deliver to the driveway at record speeds.

Amazon surely has wrestled for some time with how to get into the automotive retail category without forcing consumers to contract first with a dealer rather than stay within the Amazon walled garden. Carvana has proven how to do driveway delivery of vehicles at scale (albeit only with used cars up to now).

As Carvana works through its tests of listing other dealers' inventory on the Carvana site and scales to deliver in all fifty states, the company may become a compelling acquisition candidate for a big player such as Amazon. And if Amazon is interested, it's likely that Walmart could be a potential suitor as well.

If Carvana can figure out how to work with dealers, it will become an even more attractive acquisition target, especially given Amazon's strength in delivery logistics.

So, could this be the year that Carvana is sold to a strategic buyer? I'd be interested to see the premium needed to make that transaction happen.

Should Amazon enter automotive sales, participating dealers will have to be wary of the infamous Amazon "squeeze," where the Seattle-based company regularly unveils "private label" alternatives to compete with popular items from third parties. While I don't expect Amazon to market private-label products to compete with BMWs and Audis, Amazon could push prices down even more than we've seen from other automotive industry disruptors, in which case, there likely won't be a lot of margin left for participating dealers.

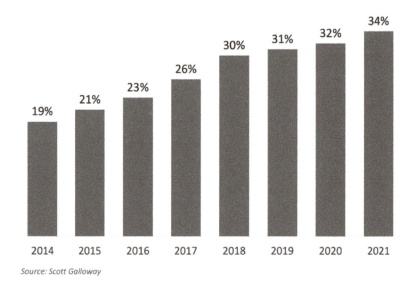

Source: Scott Galloway

Tony Rimas is bullish on the idea that Amazon will get further into the car business, but it may not be with Carvana, he says. "If I were Amazon, I'd buy AutoNation and scale it up."

Would that scaling include AutoNation's brick-and-mortar stores? Rimas isn't sure. "They could say, 'We only need five Mercedes stores to service the whole U.S.,'" in the same way that you don't need a full Amazon distribution warehouse on every corner.

How automakers perceive Amazon is another issue. If Amazon begins delivering new cars nationally, that could be very disruptive to dealerships that don't participate. Surely nonparticipating dealers will be very vocal in their opposition to Amazon helping competing dealers deliver vehicles into their market areas.

I liken Amazon to Sauron from *The Lord of the Rings:* Once they fix their eye on your product being successful, they may want to take it from you. Amazon has proven itself to be an existential threat to many merchants.

BLURRING OF LINES BETWEEN RETAIL AND WHOLESALE

When leading automotive classified-advertising site CarGurus acquired a majority of CarOffer, a back-end auction business for dealers, at a $275 million valuation in 2021, it signified a trend I expect to see accelerate in the coming years: the blurring of lines between retail and wholesale.

CarOffer allows dealers to locate and buy used vehicles through an automated bidding system. Dealers configure a "buying matrix," and CarOffer automatically fulfills that demand. The business model seems a bit adjacent to CarGurus' core consumer-facing business, but that's the point. Historic silos across the industry are being broken down; retail operations are adding wholesale activities and vice versa.

It's a big change from the pre-internet days when, once a week, a couple thousand dealers would show up at a physical auction to bid on vehicles being driven down the auction lanes. The internet has brought with it a ton of efficiencies and new business models, like CarOffer.

With CarOffer, CarGurus will now be able to provide a more end-to-end used-car solution for dealers, who can source, appraise, price, advertise and dispose of used cars on their lot. This should allow CarGurus to get deeper into dealers' wallets and to make its product stickier with less churn.

It also helps CarGurus evolve past the perception of being "just" an advertising site, and it allows the company to start participating in the vehicle transaction and to capture more gross profit per unit (GPU) sold.

CarGurus isn't quite ready to throw out its existing (and quite lucrative) business model. Rather, with CarOffer, the company has figured out how to put a supercharger on top of an already successful engine, making it that much more compelling for consumers — and dealers — to use CarGurus.

I expect competing third-party-advertising marketplaces to react to CarGurus' acquisition of CarOffer, whether through acquisitions of their own or via partnerships with players such as Manheim, ADESA or ACV Auctions.

Another trend blurring the lines between retail and wholesale is the emergence of services that enable dealers to source private seller ("for sale by owner") vehicles directly rather than needing to go to auction or dealer trades. Companies playing in this space include Drivably, Vettx, Boost Acquisition and Vehicle Acquisition Network (VAN). Fueled by the used-vehicle shortage exacerbated by COVID-19, dealers will increasingly find creative ways to source used vehicles from any and all channels.

The largest retailer of used vehicles in the U.S., CarMax, which has historically been viewed as a dealer, also runs the third-largest auction company in the country, with over seventy locations. CarMax sells more than four hundred thousand wholesale vehicles per year through these auctions.

So, is CarMax a retailer or a wholesaler — or both? Does your answer change now that it has acquired the online shopping site Edmunds?

In a very bold (and large) strategic move, Carvana acquired ADESA's fifty-six U.S. physical auction locations for $2.2 billion, making it both the second-largest used-vehicle retailer, as well as the second-largest auction company in the U.S.

During 2021, Carvana successfully acquired more vehicles from consumers than it has been able to retail. Like CarMax, Carvana requires an efficient way to dispose quickly of trade-ins and aged inventory it doesn't need. As mentioned earlier, Carvana is growing increasingly successful at convincing other dealers to list their vehicles on Carvana, as the company evolves from looking like an independent online dealership into an advertising marketplace for other dealers. With the acquisition of ADESA, Carvana will be able to offer both dealers and commercial sellers the possibility of achieving retail prices for their vehicles that otherwise would have only achieved wholesale values.

Fleet owners will continue to look for creative ways to dispose of their cars faster, more easily, more cost-effectively and at prices closer to retail.

In late 2021, for example, rental-car company Hertz announced it will use Carvana's online transaction technology and logistics network as another channel to sell used vehicles from its fleet.

CarLotz, which started its life with a used-car consignment model, went public in early 2021 via a special purpose acquisition company (SPAC) with a vision of offering fleet cars directly to consumers.

British Car Auctions (now called simply BCA) launched Cinch in 2019 as its consumer-focused used-car platform. While the U.K.-based Cinch doesn't straddle the wholesale-retail divide, the fact that it grew out of BCA, a wholesale auction business, is telling.

Cinch and parent company BCA are now a part of the Constellation Automotive Group, which also owns We Buy Any Car, the leading consumer-to-business (C2B) online car-buying platform in the U.K., providing over sixteen million used-car valuations annually and allowing some six hundred thousand consumers to sell their cars online each year.

In late 2021, Constellation acquired CarNext, a leading B2B and B2C digital used-car marketplace present in twenty-two European geographies. The combination of CarNext and Constellation creates Europe's largest digital used-car marketplace, selling more than 2.5 million cars annually for a gross merchandise value of €21 billion.

AUTO1, the wholesale business in Europe where consumers sell their used vehicles to AUTO1 subsidiary WirKaufenDeinAuto, which then markets them to dealers, has a direct-to-consumer subsidiary in Autohero. AUTO1 IPO'd in early 2021 with a market cap of over €11 billion.

As lines blur between wholesale and retail and between marketplaces and dealerships, innovation is going to happen at an increasing clip, all of which should be a net benefit to the car dealership.

THE FUTURE OF F&I

"By 2030, finance and insurance will be $100,000 per car," says Glenn Mercer. "That's a joke, of course, but for the past fifteen years, I've said that F&I can't go any higher, and then every year, we have a line heading straight up."

Here's a look at changes in F&I at six of the leading automotive groups in the U.S.

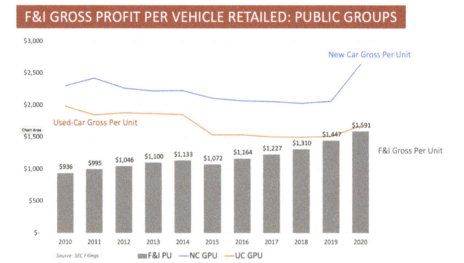

The future of finance and insurance, like everything at the dealership, is in flux.

"F&I is a bottleneck," Andrew Walser, CEO of Walser Automotive Group, told me. "People can wait up to two hours to see someone, and cash deals get pushed to the bottom of the pile because no F&I manager wants those. Compare that with an Apple Store, where every salesperson has a checkout device."

Dealers have long had a love-hate relationship with F&I.

"Dealers don't love their F&I departments," Walser continues. "They're mostly staffed by mercenaries who go from store to store and get paid a lot."

Gordon explains the mercenary analogy.

"The F&I manager is one of the highest paid positions in a dealership because they control so many of the levers around profitability," he notes. "It's a revered position. Dealers are always looking to hire more experienced F&I managers with track records of high product penetration and profitability per vehicle."

As a result, F&I managers are frequently picked off by other dealers.

"If dealers had a solution to replace that person with technology, most dealers would do it, if only to eliminate the bottleneck, but they're afraid to do anything because they're making so much money on F&I," adds Walser, whose company FUSE Autotech aims to do just that.

"We want to make everyone in the dealership a cashier," he quips.

Indeed, after service, F&I is the most lucrative part of the dealership today. It's the F&I manager who will try to convince a buyer to add additional insurance products, like vehicle service contracts, or more accessories, like a roof rack or tinted windows.

In 2020, AutoNation reported earning more than $1 billion in F&I revenue — around $1,600 per car.

Nineteen dealership groups in the U.S. reported F&I revenue above $100 million. F&I revenue increased 13% between 2015 and 2018, according to NADA.

But now, the internet and transparency threaten to upend this cash cow.

"Dealers get only about half the F&I revenue when it's sold online," Chase Fraser told me. "A company that figures out how to do F&I online and gets it right will be huge."

Online transparency will allow consumers to cross-shop F&I products in the future, which will put additional pressure on dealer profit margins.

For example, it would probably annoy a lot of people to learn that the insurance product a dealer steered them into had a profit margin of 400%, or that the dealer only had to pay $150 for the $900 extended maintenance product sold to the consumer.

Enter the Consumer Financial Protection Bureau (CFPB), often the car buyer's best (and only) friend.

In 2020, for example, the CFPB found that Lobel Financial Corporation "engaged in unfair practices" when, following a late payment, it billed consumers extra for its loss damage waiver (LDW) product without actually providing the product. When customers later needed repairs, Lobel would deny their claims.

Lobel was ordered to pay $1,345,224 to four thousand harmed customers and a $100,000 civil money penalty.

In 2021, the CFPB took aim at another lender, California Auto Finance, for illegally charging interest for late payment on its LDW product.

Creating branded F&I products may be another way forward. Carvana and CarMax both operate their own financial institutions to originate loans, and Carvana has its own F&I products under the "SilverRock" name.

Smart dealers know that it's just a matter of time, and they can't fight transparency or maintain their stranglehold around F&I forever. This genie is already well on its way out of the bottle.

NEW BUSINESS MODELS AND CONFIGURATIONS

As changes roil the industry, what will happen to dealers?

The first and most obvious change: The big players will get bigger and will absorb smaller, poorly operated dealers to drive efficiencies and compete with the Carvanas and Lithias of the industry.

Standalone dealers will have trouble. Mom-and-pop dealerships may pretty much cease to exist.

"Smaller dealers will need to consolidate operations to survive," notes industry consultant and president of AutoProfit Ed French. "Fringe 'dirt lot' dealers are dead."

And while life may be good now, single operators should already be thinking, "Is it time to sell to a larger group with multiple stores?"

Even well-established brick-and-mortar brands such as CarMax are experimenting with hybrid models that incorporate omnichannel sales software.

For CarMax, it's less about shifting to 100% online purchases with driveway deliveries and more about enabling customers to shop the way they want — entirely at home, or starting at home and finalizing their purchase at a physical dealership.

I once had a professor in college who said that the best way to win a game is not to simply be a participant, but to dictate the rules of the game. If a dealer can't dictate the rules, it may be time to say, "I can't play anymore." It may be time to move on.

This is where companies like Tesla have the advantage.

Elon Musk is rewriting the rules, tipping the scales in his favor.

Electrification, fewer service opportunities and over-the-air updates are threats that will keep dealers up at night. When autonomy hits and a good chunk of vehicle ownership shifts to fleets, dealers will need to ask themselves, "What role do I play in the industry?"

When enough uncertainty mounts, dealers will start to think about when to get out.

"In twenty years, dealerships will be borderline unrecognizable," adds venture capitalist Bill Cariss. "Sales will be all online, and dealerships will be more like storefronts. As when you go into the Apple Store to replace your AirPods, you'll go to the dealership for your transportation mobility needs. Maybe there's a Genius Bar. It could even be a cool place to hang out, a community of sorts."

That makes sense to mobility investor Mike Granoff.

"Apple reimagined retail for the brand and product and services. Of course, things in mobility will get reimagined too," he told me.

Ed French agrees.

"Dealers will have to become more boutique," he says. "The dealer experience will become very concierge, like fine dining. Dealers will need more of a concierge level of service if they're going to survive. They'll have to put the white gloves on. But that could lead to larger margins because people will pay a premium for a concierge type of service."

French anticipates dealers stocking no more than ten to fifteen cars on their lots in the future, "so you get a chance to at least look at the car.

The days of the Ford dealership with one thousand new cars on the ground . . . that ship has sailed."

Moreover, French suggests we need to imagine how the millions of high schoolers who will soon become drivers will shop for cars.

"We're still complaining about the changes with Gen Z, but there's a whole group coming behind them that's grown up on AI, personalization, drones," he stresses. "They're not going to read a two-year-old *People* magazine while waiting for their car. That doesn't exist in their minds. You've got to look not at where we are today but at where the 16-year-olds are heading. What will the retail automotive experience offer them?"

"There will be no need to have cars sitting on the lot or to have inventory," speculates Dennis Clark. "Asset-light businesses always win out. I see dealers pivoting — twenty years from now, they won't be in the business of selling cars."

Walser describes the less creative dealers as being "stuck in a time machine."

Artificial intelligence and process automation may help dealers survive — by reducing headcount. It will be particularly relevant in the business development center (BDC), that division of a dealership that handles lead generation. Instead of a dozen employees in the back room returning calls and emails and text messages, AI can prequalify the leads without human intervention so that only the most relevant ones warrant a direct response. That results in more efficiency and a better consumer experience to boot.

Again, that's more likely to happen at large dealerships than at independent ones.

"It's become too expensive to run a single operation in today's economic climate, even with profits as good as they are now," says French. "An independent operator in a long-term family business where everything is already paid for — it's a really nice job, but it's not a business. In the next five years, we'll lose half of those small dealers. They'll go the way of local hardware stores competing with Home Depot."

Of the eighteen thousand franchise dealers currently operating in the U.S., how many will be left standing in the next five, ten or twenty years?

Will the future of automotive retailing support all eighteen thousand? How about five thousand? Or fewer?

One thing is for certain: Dealerships have been incredibly creative and resilient, evolving the business model as quickly as disruptive elements have been strewn across their routes. I like to think of a well-run dealership as a water-filled balloon: Squeeze one area, and another expands, compensating for the area that's being squeezed.

A diversified dealership can have up to seven healthy P&Ls, which naturally hedge operations against pressures in any single area of the business.

It can look like this dealer floor plan:

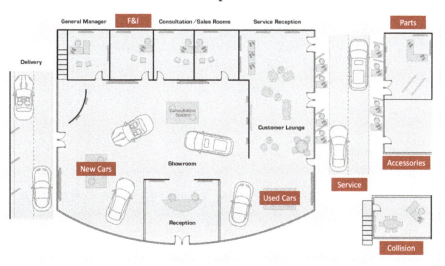

While change is inevitably coming, dealers have the time, energy and frame of mind to make thoughtful decisions rather than react rashly; those who want out have the opportunity to make that move, and those who want to consolidate can drive on that path too.

It's a confusing time to own a dealership. But just as cars are not going away but are evolving, the same is certainly true for the way dealers can, will and must operate.

PRACTICAL STEPS

We've come to the end of the book.

To recap, over the course of the last nine chapters, we've considered eight key themes affecting the future of automotive retail:

1. **Consumer preferences and the convenience economy** — How will the "Amazonification of car retailing" play out among the Carvanas, Vrooms and Lithias? Will Gen Zers even get their driver's licenses in the future, or are Uber and Lyft enough? Does convenience trump money? Who needs to visit a dealership with driveway delivery and seven-day money-back test-drive guarantees?
2. **Power source** — Will it be electric, hydrogen or something unexpected? Will gasoline-powered cars be 100% banned? When?
3. **Vehicle production** — Can the internet, AI and big data make OEMs more effective at determining which regions and which consumers want which cars?
4. **Vehicle ownership** — Will consumers still buy cars when they're 100% autonomous? Will subscriptions become the rule rather than the exception even before then?
5. **Autonomy** — Will self-driving cars prove to be the biggest disruption of all? When will they hit the streets and in what configurations? (Robo-taxis, self-driving trucks?) Is true Level 5 autonomy achievable?
6. **Connectivity** — Who wins when cars can be updated over the air? Will OEMs and dealers fight over who gets the revenue? How can we ensure privacy over consumer data?
7. **Service** — As electric vehicles promise less repairs, how can dealerships add new revenue generators to the service department? Will the complexities of replacing high-tech windshields be key to preventing consumers from giving their business to Eddie's Garage? Will consumers demand brake

changes in their driveways?
8. **The future of the dealership** — Is it time to sell? To consolidate? How is the blurring of the lines between retail and wholesale affecting the industry? How can dealers deal with disruption? Can trust be fostered? Will Amazon buy Carvana or AutoNation?

I'd like to conclude our exploration into the future of automotive retail with a review of some of the practical steps dealers might consider, steps that we've identified over the course of this book.

PRACTICAL NEXT STEPS

1. Identify New Revenue Streams
2. Reduce Costs
3. Build Scale Through Acquisition
4. Embrace Consumer-Centric Online Experiences
5. Anticipate Disruption
6. Build Infrastructure Now
7. Focus on Convenience as a Differentiator

1. **Identify new revenue streams.** Margin compression is likely to return with a vengeance, so dealers must proactively explore new revenue opportunities. Many of these will be in their service departments — repairing increasingly complex vehicles, lidar/radar/camera calibration, collision repair, late-night charging and car washes. Aftermarket parts and accessories, as

well as over-the-air software upgrades, will constitute a potential and significant source of new revenue. Innovation in new-vehicle subscription models may provide additional sources of income.

2. **Reduce costs.** As margins become compressed, dealers will need to focus on cutting expenses and increasing efficiencies. Staff is a dealership's largest line item. According to NADA, SG&A (selling, general and administrative) expenses — the vast majority of which is labor — runs close to 90% of a dealership's gross margin. (During 2021, the number dropped to just north of 70% but is expected to jump back to the higher figure in the long term.) Artificial intelligence and process automation will play an important role here, and I forecast that we are going to see a wave of new technology solutions that help dealers automate processes and/or focus on stabilizing the workforce. Actively and deliberately repurposing existing staff to more profitable and growing areas of the business will be another important factor.

3. **Build scale through acquisition.** If you're in a position to acquire competitors, now would be a good time to do so. If you're a small, single-rooftop owner, it might be time to consider seeking out someone to acquire your dealership. In a world increasingly dominated by retailers who embrace a dramatically better consumer experience, the migration of consumers from internal combustion engine vehicles to electric and to cars that can be updated over the air will be the big players. How do you position yourself to have the size and scale to compete in this environment?

4. **Embrace consumer-centric online experiences.** Consumer expectations are being set in areas outside of automotive by large technology companies such as Amazon, Netflix, Apple and Facebook. The automotive shopper of the future will expect a new level of convenience — for example, wanting to conduct most, if not all, of the automotive transaction online. An

increasing number of shoppers are sure to expect their vehicle to be delivered to their driveway, with no human interaction at a dealership involved.

5. **Anticipate disruption.** Netflix disrupted Blockbuster into bankruptcy. The iPhone disrupted established players such as Nokia, BlackBerry and Motorola. Then the internet disrupted everything. I've attempted in this book to forecast some of the key disruptions for the coming years, but the nature of disruptions is that they tend to get disrupted themselves!

6. **Build infrastructure now.** Can today's power grid handle the demands of an all-electric vehicle world? Can batteries be tweaked to provide even greater range — or faster charges? Will in-road charging be a solution? Dealers cannot necessarily influence these things, but other tech advances should be top of mind, such as building the right EV charging infrastructure that accommodates future electric models and helping consumers make good choices about the chargers they will need at home.

7. **Focus on convenience as a differentiator.** Curate experiences your customers will love. Whether that's an Apple Store-esque Genius bar, a cool community hangout or free gourmet donuts and cold-brew coffee for those waiting for a tire rotation, delight your customers, and they'll keep coming back.

BACK TO THE FUTURE

Little Ruthie and Joel were already awake when Monty and Emerson's VR massage alarm went off. Gone was the abrupt clang of old-school clocks; in 2050, waking up could be as pleasant as a cool breeze with a light touch.

Ruthie and Joel were giggling together in the kitchen where they had whipped up some pancakes — or rather, Joel had memorized which button to press on the 3D breakfast printer.

With the morning routine well under control, Monty eye-swiped right on his augmented reality glasses to call his car and was soon on his autonomous commute, reviewing the previous week's sales figures and checking what was on his calendar for the day.

"I've got the candles for Joel's birthday cake," his Volvo chirped. "They're in the delivery frunk. We can pick up the chocolate ganache tonight."

Monty wished his mother could have seen all this; she would have loved knowing her grandchildren would never miss out on cake — and more importantly, that life was calmer, more efficient and, despite it all, still profitable. That Monty was still in business was an achievement. As owner of one of the few remaining independent dealerships, Monty had kept his mother's dream going and carved out a niche for high-quality service at a reasonable price.

Monty's car pulled into a drive-through tent set up adjacent to the Boston Chowda Co. outlet at Faneuil Hall.

"Hey, I didn't say I wanted soup!" Monty protested, until he saw the flashing digital cardboard square nestled in a crevice of the soup's insulated PlastiMesh container.

Monty tapped the top.

"Have a great week!" the card sang out as holographic images of Emerson, Joel and Ruthie danced around the front of the vehicle.

Monty chuckled. He had faced the future of automotive retail full-on and survived to greet another day, with gusto and support from his loving family, who always knew when a little pick-me-up could make all the difference.

Monty took a sip of soup through the integrated Turbostraw (yes, sipping soup through a mechanized straw was a thing in 2050). Ah, creamy tomato, his favorite.

As his vehicle approached the dealership, Monty straightened his paisley bolo, adjusted his AR glasses and switched on his neural implant.

Now, let's get out there and sell some cars!

EPILOGUE

THE CALF-PATH

In 1895, the American poet Sam Walter Foss wrote "The Calf-Path," which addressed how we human beings fall victim to repeating ineffective patterns through our fealty to convention. That loyalty eventually becomes carved in stone.

This attitude is as relevant to the automotive industry as to any other, and it can trap dealers and OEMs. ("We've always done it that way!")

"The Calf-Path" serves as a fitting conclusion to our look at the future of automotive retailing, and I am happy to present it to you here.

I.

One day through the primeval wood
A calf walked home as good calves should;
But made a trail all bent askew,
A crooked trail as all calves do.
Since then three hundred years have fled,
And I infer the calf is dead.

II.

But still he left behind his trail,
And thereby hangs my moral tale.
The trail was taken up next day,
By a lone dog that passed that way;
And then a wise bell-wether sheep
Pursued the trail o'er vale and steep,
And drew the flock behind him, too,
As good bell-wethers always do.
And from that day, o'er hill and glade.
Through those old woods a path was made.

III.

And many men wound in and out,
And dodged, and turned, and bent about,
And uttered words of righteous wrath,
Because 'twas such a crooked path;
But still they followed — do not laugh —
The first migrations of that calf,
And through this winding wood-way stalked
Because he wobbled when he walked.

IV.

This forest path became a lane,
That bent and turned and turned again;
This crooked lane became a road,
Where many a poor horse with his load
Toiled on beneath the burning sun,
And traveled some three miles in one.
And thus a century and a half
They trod the footsteps of that calf.

V.

The years passed on in swiftness fleet,
The road became a village street;
And this, before men were aware,
A city's crowded thoroughfare.
And soon the central street was this
Of a renowned metropolis;
And men two centuries and a half,
Trod in the footsteps of that calf.

VI.

Each day a hundred thousand rout
Followed the zigzag calf about
And o'er his crooked journey went
The traffic of a continent.
A hundred thousand men were led,
By one calf near three centuries dead.
They followed still his crooked way,
And lost one hundred years a day;
For thus such reverence is lent,
To well-established precedent.

VII.

A moral lesson this might teach
Were I ordained and called to preach;
For men are prone to go it blind
Along the calf-paths of the mind,
And work away from sun to sun,
To do what other men have done.
They follow in the beaten track,
And out and in, and forth and back,
And still their devious course pursue,
To keep the path that others do.
They keep the path a sacred groove,
Along which all their lives they move.
But how the wise old wood gods laugh,
Who saw the first primeval calf.
Ah, many things this tale might teach —
But I am not ordained to preach.

ACKNOWLEDGEMENTS

I am grateful to have stumbled across the automotive industry, almost by chance. Thanks to my high school buddy John Scharf for that serendipitous call one evening in late 2009, encouraging me to apply for the newly created position of technology manager at Toronto Auto Auction.

This industry has been extremely generous to me, and I want to express my sincere thanks to all the folks who have encouraged and supported my career and personal growth, who helped define me as a person and who have been along this journey with me.

I would like to thank both Brad Hart and Ruth Hart Stephens for offering me that first job in the automotive industry, and then for selflessly encouraging me to make the move from Canada to the United States.

Thank you, Gordon Warren, for spurring me to work just a little bit harder than everyone else.

Thank you, Michael Lasini, for encouraging me to pursue further education and always having faith in my abilities.

I'd like to express my gratitude to Patrick Noonan for challenging all of us, instilling a sense of rigor and pride in our work and providing the environment to truly explore our limits.

Thank you, Dean Eisner, for being so very generous with your time at a point when I was considering leaving the industry. And for opening up about your own past as a reflection and road map for me to understand and follow.

Thanks to Mike Langhorne for taking a chance on a kid early in his career and entrusting him to represent a multibillion-dollar company overseas.

Sincere thanks to Chip Perry for taking a chance on me for a role that I wasn't prepared for and teaching me the power of having more faith in a person than that person may have in himself.

Thank you, Dale Pollak, for being so generous with your time and enlightening me about how great businesses are built.

Thank you to my investors in Automotive Ventures for placing your confidence in me.

Thanks, too, to the limited partners in our VC fund for taking a chance on a first-time fund manager.

Thank you, Stella, for your unwavering support as I jumped from one entrepreneurial venture to the next.

Thanks go out to Rafa, Lucy, Oscar, Luna, Henry, Pippa, Remi, Charles and Lamb Chop for making me a better person.

And, finally, I'm most thankful for my mother, for being the most inspirational person in my life. I couldn't have asked for a better role model who, by example, taught me the secret to life: gratitude, generosity and grace.

I would be remiss without expressing my sincere thanks to Brian Blum, who has been my collaborator throughout the entire book-writing process. You are such an amazing human being, and I honestly could never have even envisioned this thing coming together without you as a partner. May this be the first of many more projects into the future.

NOTES

CHAPTER ONE

The predictions in this chapter are speculative, of course, but the conclusions are based on the research presented in the rest of this book.

The "No Soup for You" reference is from season seven, episode two of *Seinfeld,* which aired on November 2, 1995.

Elon Musk spoke about the "Tesla Bot" at the company's 2021 AI Day.

Boston Chowda Co. is a real soup and sandwich shop. I hope it will still be around in 2050!

CHAPTER TWO

The data on Carvana's stock price and market cap comes from *Seeking Alpha* (June 29, 2021) and other business publications.

Ray Furchgott's reporting on millennials and car buying is taken from his *New York Times* article "Happy to Shun Showrooms, Millennials Storm the Car Market" (June 17, 2021).

The *AIM Group Marketplaces Report* states that 80% of car deals will have some digital elements, and includes interviews with the Avondale Group's Kennedy Gibson, Anderson Auto's Dan Sayer, and Joe Chura, CEO of Dealer Inspire. The surveys from CarGurus and Cox Automotive are also in this report.

Deloitte's reasons why consumers might not buy online comes from its *Global Automotive Consumer Study 2021.*

Paul Walser's quote appeared in the *Wall Street Journal* article "Everything Must Go! The American Car Dealership Is for Sale" (September 11, 2021).

Background on Lithia comes from Jackie Charniga's *Automotive News* piece, "Lithia Plans Buying Spree to Become $50 Billion Retailer by 2025" (May 3, 2021).

Maryann Keller's white paper titled *Consumer Benefits of the Dealer Franchise System* originally appeared as part of NADA's "Get the Facts" series.

Andy Bruce told the *Telegraph,* "People would rather go to the dentist than a car dealer" (August 15, 2015).

José Muñoz told Laurence Iliff at *Automotive News* that EVs will only need one-third the amount of servicing as ICE vehicles in the article "Fast-Changing Retail Landscape Strains Factory-Dealer Relations" (June 7, 2021).

Herbert Diess's quote about how long it will take the industry to transform comes from the *Wall Street Journal* article "How Electric, Self-Driving Cars and Ride-Hailing Will Transform the Car Industry" (April 23, 2021).

This chapter includes my personal interviews with Cliff Banks, Ed French, Andrew Gordon, Mike Granoff and Andrew Walser.

CHAPTER THREE

The figure from the Environmental Defense Fund on pollution was cited in the article "How Much Air Pollution Comes from Cars?" by Linda C. Brinson and Francisco Guzman on *HowStuffWorks* (July 7, 2021).

The statistics on EV uptake and resistance from E&Y, BCG, *Bloomberg,* OC&C and McKinsey were compiled from several sources, including Brett Haensel's *Bloomberg* article, "Electric Vehicles Seen Reaching Sales Supremacy By 2033, Faster than Expected" (June 23, 2021), Alexa St. John's *Automotive News* piece, "EVs to Account for More than Half of Light Vehicles Sold Globally by 2026" (April 20, 2021) and the OC&C Automotive Disruption Speedometer survey.

Larry Vellequette brought us the statistic from the Automotive News Research & Data Center in his *Automotive News* article, "The

Disconnect in Our Electric Grid" (July 19, 2021). His piece also quotes Dustin Krause and David Reuter and discusses the 2,000-megawatt power plant near Cleveland.

The YouGov poll on "What's Stopping Americans from Buying Electric Cars?" was published on October 23, 2020.

Jay Leno told CNBC's Emily DeCiccio, "The electric car is here to stay despite Chevy Bolt recalls" (September 16, 2021).

There are many more details on GM's EV1 project in Chris Paine's 2006 documentary, "Who Killed the Electric Car?"

More on why Bob Lutz decided to back the EV1 can be found in *Totaled,* Brian Blum's 2017 book on the demise of Israeli electric car startup Better Place.

Mary Barra appeared on the December 2, 2020, episode of *Freakonomics Radio,* "Is It Too Late for General Motors to Go Electric?"

Scott Painter spoke to the *AIM Group Marketplaces Report* on Tesla, Fair and NextCar in January 2020.

You can find pictures of Ford's "frunk" in the *InsideEVs* article "Ford F-150 Lightning Will Have the Largest Trunk in the Industry" (November 16, 2021).

Ford's decision to begin taking orders for the F-150 was reported by Steve Hanley for *CleanTechnica*: "Ford Ends F-150 Lightning Reservations, Says It Needs More Batteries" (December 10, 2021).

Jim Farley's and Darren Palmer's quotes on EVs at Ford come from an article on *The Car Connection* website, "Ford's EV Strategy Shows How Much Can Change in a Decade" (July 26, 2021).

The Verge reported on Tesla's ill-fated battery swap program, "Tesla Sounds Ready to Pull the Plug on Promised Battery-Swap Technology" (June 9, 2015).

NIO's battery swap success was reported in the *EVAdoption* article "What's the Future of Oil Changing Shops When Cars Go Electric?" (July 8, 2020).

NIO's plans to test Level 4 autonomous vehicles in Tel Aviv were covered by the Israeli business publication *Globes,* "NIO Cars Arriving in Israel for Mobileye Robo-Taxi Trials" (June 24, 2021).

Electric cars in Norway received coverage in this article in the *Guardian*: "Electric Cars Rise to Record 54% Market Share in Norway" (January 5, 2021).

Adam Simms, Justin Gasman, Anders Gustafsson, Jorge Gutierrez and Ernie Norcross were all quoted by Urvaksh Karkaria and Hannah Lutz in their *Automotive News* article, "Dealers Concerned Margins Will Shrink" (June 7, 2021).

We learned about tires and maintenance for EVs in this *TechCrunch* piece: "Electric Vehicles Are Changing the Future of Auto Maintenance" (March 3, 2020).

Blake Shaffer knows about electric vehicles' weight problems. He told *Fast Company*'s Adele Peters all about it in the October 2021 article "Electric Vehicles Have a Weight Problem."

PHEVs are not AutoForecast Solutions' cup of tea, per this article on *Reuters*: "Once 'Green' Plug-in Hybrid Cars Suddenly Look Like Dinosaurs in Europe" (April 12, 2021).

Chris Reynolds' talks in Washington on slowing down EV sales and David Friedman's comments on hydrogen were reported in the *New York Times* article "Toyota Led on Clean Cars. Now Critics Say It Works to Delay Them" (July 25, 2021).

Dave Gardner's comments come from the *USA Today* article "Honda to Reveal Prologue Electric SUV" by Nathan Bomey (June 28, 2021).

Larry Burns is quoted in an article from *Deloitte Insights Magazine* on "The Power of 'And'" (January 18, 2019).

Benchmark Mineral Intelligence reports extensively on lithium-ion batteries at benchmarkminerals.com.

Davide Castelvecchi explored the topic "Electric Cars and Batteries: How Will the World Produce Enough?" in *Nature* (August 17, 2021).

Sasha Lekach reported that Tesla will open its Superchargers to non-Tesla EVs on *Mashable* (July 26, 2021).

There's more on StoreDot in this 2016 article in *Israel21c*, "Israeli Company Promises a 5-Minute Recharge for Your Electric Car" (May 2, 2009).

We learned about ABB's fifteen-minute EV charge plans from *Auto News Europe*, "The Swiss company says the Terra 360 can fully charge any electric car in 15 minutes" (September 30, 2021).

Bloomberg has more on gallium nitride in "Silicon Valley Answer to the EV Question Calls for Less Silicon" (September 29, 2021).

Henry Graber wonders in *Slate,* "Where the Heck Are We Going to Charge All of the Electric Cars?" (October 28, 2021).

The *Good News Network* reported on in-road charging from Magment, Siemens and Electreon in "German Company Makes Concrete to Charge Electric Vehicles from Roads" (August 24, 2021). Oren Ezer spoke to Yaacov Benmeleh at *Bloomberg Businessweek* for the article "Israeli Startup Sees Electricity Paving Road to the Future" (July 6, 2021). And Khurram Afridi was interviewed by *Business Insider* on May 9, 2021, for the article "New Electric Vehicle Charging Research Could Allow Drivers to Power Their Cars as They Drive on the Highway."

"Has the electric car's moment arrived at last?" Sam Ricketts and Kristin Dziczek think so in a January 2021 *National Geographic* piece of the same name.

This chapter includes my personal interviews with Reilly Brennan, Dennis Clark, Mike Granoff and Jay Vijayan.

CHAPTER FOUR

Incentives equaling $2,065 per vehicle come from research conducted by Automotive Ventures. New car incentives are typically around $5,000 per vehicle. The $30 billion to $50 billion figure is based on incentives being applied to fifteen million vehicles sold per year at retail.

Håkan Samuelsson shared his views on build-to-order with Urvaksh Karkaria of *Automotive News* in "Volvo's Samuelsson: A Good Time for Change" (September 20, 2021).

Doug Betts emphasizes "build to order" in Steven Finlay's article "Automakers Urged to Stop Building 'Unicorns'" for *WardsAuto* (May

22, 2020). WardsAuto also features an article by Brian Finkelmeyer, "Margin for Error Just Got Smaller in New-Car Operations" (June 29, 2020).

Is 3D-printing automotive parts really like Build-A-Bear? Read what John Rogers has to say in the *New York Times* article "A 3-D Printed Car, Ready for the Road" (January 16, 2015).

Daniel Barel explains how REE operates in the article "Israeli Startup Is Totally Reinventing How Cars Are Built," *Israel21c* (September 29, 2019).

Pat Gelsinger's figure that premium cars will have five times more chips than they did in 2010 has been widely reported, including here: "Mobileye to Launch Driverless Taxis in 2022," *Globes* (September 8, 2021).

Huei Peng gave his prediction on "Tesla chips" to *Wired* in the article "Why Tesla Is Designing Chips to Train Its Self-Driving Tech" (September 7, 2021).

Patrick Penfield spoke to *Recode* for the article "The Chip Shortage Is Getting Worse" (August 5, 2021).

J.D. Power reported that the 2021 cost for incentives is $2,065 per vehicle (July 2021).

Peter Lanzavecchia was cited by Laurence Iliff in his *Automotive News* article, "Fast-Changing Retail Landscape Strains Factory-Dealer Relations" (June 7, 2021).

The *Los Angeles Times* reported on GM's aborted consolidation plans in "In Consolidation Move, GM to Buy Area Dealerships" (December 2, 1997).

Ford's unsuccessful experiment was covered in Tim Keenan's *WardsAuto* articles, "Ford Gets Out of the Dealership Game; Leaves Dealerships to Dealers" (June 26, 2001) and "Ford No Longer a Collection Agency" (August 1, 2001).

Laurie Winslow wrote about Ford's discontinuation of its "Auto Collections" initiative for *Tulsa World* in the article, "Ford Hits Brakes, Agrees to Sell Auto Collection" (June 27, 2001).

Dan McNichol and Ann Blakney spoke to Stewart Deck of *Computerworld* way back in February 2001.

The Scali Rasmussen law firm covered the Volvo subscription program uproar in an August 2020 post on the company's website, "Volvo Forced to Terminate 'Subscription' Program in California."

Dimitris Psillakis spoke to *Automotive News* for the article "Dealers Concerned Margins Will Shrink" (June 7, 2021).

This chapter includes my personal interviews with Cliff Banks, Reilly Brennan, Chase Fraser, Ed French, Andrew Gordon, Dave Paratore, Tony Rimas, Jay Vijayan and Andrew Walser.

CHAPTER FIVE

Travis Kalanick got his "dude" on during a talk at the Code Conference 2014, reported in the *Verge* article "Uber Will Eventually Replace All Its Drivers with Self-Driving Cars" (May 28, 2014).

Larry Burns spoke to Derek Pankratz for *Deloitte Insights Magazine* in January 2021.

Scott Painter called vehicle subscription an "antidote" in the January 14, 2020, issue of the *AIM Group Marketplaces Report.* In that same issue, Hans Christ, Marta Daina, Henrik Littorin, Lea Miggiano, Maximilian Renoth, Hilde Sommerstad and Aaron Tan spoke about car subscriptions. Much of the background on Fair.com and Painter comes from that same issue and from Greg Spencer's reporting for the *AIM Group Marketplaces Report* in August 2021.

Capgemini's estimate of subscription interest was published on January 24, 2020, under the title, "Hot or Not? What Do Consumers Really Want in Terms of Car Subscription Services?"

Jerry Lewis and Stanley Kubrick had their interaction when Kubrick was editing *2001: A Space Odyssey* in 1968.

Adam Jonas's comments on a potential "Apple Car" were cited by Clark Schultz for *Seeking Alpha* (November 19, 2021).

Details on Hyundai's hybrid subscription option can be found in the *Automotive News* article "Unlike Most Asian Rivals That Have Been Ho-Hum on Electric Vehicles, Hyundai Says It's All In" (May 31, 2021).

The automotive website *Jalopnik's* Lawrence Hodge detailed all the subscription service programs that have gone bust in "Once Hailed as the Next Evolution in Car Buying, Car Subscription Services Are All but Gone" (April 15, 2021).

Care by Volvo's U.K. statistics come from Volvo Cars UK (September 2, 2021).

This chapter includes my personal interviews with Reilly Brennan and Chase Fraser.

CHAPTER SIX

Mobileye's robo-taxi plans in Israel and Germany were reported in articles appearing in *Globes* and the *Jerusalem Post*, among others, on September 8, 2021.

The five levels of autonomy are described well in Jessica Shea Choksey and Christian Wardlaw's May 5, 2021, article for J.D. Power, "Levels of Autonomous Driving, Explained."

Morgan Stanley's predictions are taken from Clark Schultz's article, "Apple's Potential Autonomous Car Is Called the Ultimate EV Bear Case by Morgan Stanley," for *Seeking Alpha* (November 19, 2021).

Larry Burns spoke about "situational awareness," the "epidemic" in deaths and injuries from car crashes, and people wanting to own their own cars, even if autonomous, in his *Deloitte Insights Magazine* interview on "The Power of 'And'" (January 18, 2019).

Amnon Shashua's quotes on autonomous driving in this chapter are taken from Eytan Avriel's extensive profile of the Mobileye CEO in *Haaretz*, "Elon Musk, Behind You: Israeli Self-Driving Cars to Hit the Road Next Year" (April 8, 2021).

The figures on how many collisions occur per mile and how many autonomous vehicles are currently on the roads come from "35

Statistics About Self-Driving Vehicles" by Cem Dilmegani on the AIMultiple blog (July 5, 2021).

The Uber accident that killed Elaine Herzberg was widely reported at the time. One good source is the BBC article "Uber Halts Self-Driving Car Tests After Death" (March 20, 2018). The *New York Times* reported on the two men killed in Texas. The BBC also covered Robbie Miller's warning in "Uber Told Self-Drive Cars Unsafe Days Before Accident" (December 13, 2018). Jason Levine's quote on autonomous vehicle safety can be found in the *National Law Review* article "The Dangers of Driverless Cars (May 5, 2021). The University of Michigan study was reported on the *Government Technology* site: "First Driverless Car Crash: Autonomous Vehicles Crash More but Injuries Are Less Serious" (October 30, 2015).

Alex Kopestinsky compiled the statistics on how comfortable consumers would be in a self-driving vehicle in the article "25 Astonishing Self-Driving Car Statistics for 2021" for the PolicyAdvice website (April 29, 2021).

Much of the data on hacking autonomous vehicles, including quotes from Steve Wernikoff, Rebecca Chaney, Chuck Brokish and Chris Urmson, can be found in the article "Autonomous Cars Low on a Hacker's Hit List, for Now," published in *Automotive World* (October 2, 2020).

Mark Fields's predictions were covered by Ina Fried in the *Vox* article "Ford CEO Mark Fields Says Fully Autonomous Cars Could Hit Roads in Four Years" (November 18, 2015).

Jesse Levinson's comments on Zoox and rainy Seattle comes from the *Business Insider* article "Amazon's Zoox Is Testing Self-Driving Cars in Seattle So They Can Learn to Cope with Lots of Rain" (October 19, 2021).

Herbert Diess's comments on smart cars as a game changer were reported by Christopher Steitz and Jan Schwartz in the *Reuters* article "Volkswagen CEO: Smart Cars, Not E-Cars, Are 'Game Changer'" (September 5, 2021).

Reuters also reported on robo-taxis in Dubai: "Cruise to Deploy Robo-Taxis in Dubai from 2023" (April 12, 2021).

Bloomberg's reporting on Apple's "Project Titan" can be found in the article "Apple Accelerates Work on Car Project, Aiming for Fully Autonomous Vehicle" (November 18, 2021). It was also *Bloomberg* that interviewed Tim Cook in 2017 in the article "Tim Cook Says Apple Focused on Autonomous Systems in Cars Push" (June 13, 2017). And another *Bloomberg* article ("Hyundai Walks Back Confirmation It's in Talks Over Apple Car") reported that Hyundai was not in discussions with Apple (January 7, 2021).

You can read more about Gatik's partnership with Isuzu on the Modern Shipping website: "Gatik, Isuzu to Partner on Autonomous Truck Platform" (April 6, 2021).

The Hill's Mychael Schnell wrote about FedEx's plans in "FedEx Launches Autonomous Truck Routes" (September 22, 2021).

More on Nuro's pizza deliveries in *Business Insider*: "Self-Driving Delivery Startup Nuro Is Partnering With Domino's to Deliver Pizzas" (April 12, 2021).

The OC&C data on autonomous driving comes from the company's Automotive Disruption Speedometer survey.

Elon Musk told Cade Metz he was "highly confident" that self-driving cars are coming as early as 2021 in the *New York Times* article "Tesla Sells 'Full Self-Driving,' but What Is It Really?" (August 20, 2021).

This chapter includes my personal interviews with Cliff Banks, Reilly Brennan, Dennis Clark, Chase Fraser, Ed French, Andrew Gordon, Glenn Mercer, Tony Rimas and Jay Vijayan.

CHAPTER SEVEN

Wired reported on the 2013 Tesla Model S fire in "Tesla Tweaks Model S Wirelessly as Feds Investigate Battery Fires" (November 13, 2013).

Jake Fisher's *Consumer Reports* investigation is titled "Tesla Model 3 Gets CR Recommendation After Braking Update" (May 30, 2018).

How many lines of software code are in a car? Bosch says one hundred million *(Automotive World,* July 21, 2020). McKinsey suggests it's closer to three hundred million ("Ready for Inspection — The Automotive Aftermarket in 2030," June 2018). The figure on "25 gigabytes of data per hour" and that 58% of consumers would follow their vehicle's recommendation for a repair shop come from the same McKinsey report.

Jim Farley spoke to *Automotive News*'s Michael Martinez about recurring revenue streams in "Ford's Jim Farley Aims to Build 'Always-On' Relationships" (August 30, 2021).

Oliver Blume's comment on OTA updates at Porsche were made to Jim Holder in the *Autocar* article "New Porsche Taycan 'Set to Rewrite Performance EV Benchmarks'" (September 9, 2019).

Randell Suba reports on Tesla's 120+ OTA updates for the Tesla 3 in "Tesla Finds Fountain of Youth as Model 3 'Ages' with 124 OTA Software Products," *Teslarati* (January 20, 2020).

IHS's estimate on OTA cost savings was reported in *Fortune:* "How Automakers Will Save $35 Billion by 2022" (September 4, 2015). ABI Research's figures were published by the consulting firm itself in "ABI Research Anticipates Accelerated Adoption of Automotive Software Over-the-Air Updates" (March 15, 2016).

The McKinsey report "Unlocking the Full Life-Cycle Value from Connected-Car Data" was published on February 11, 2021.

Brian Benstock's comments come from the *Automotive News* 2018 webinar, "Do's and Don'ts of a Frictionless Customer Experience."

SBD Automotive's figures on trustworthiness and connected cars in Europe was published in February 2020.

Guidehouse published its *Cost Consideration Guide* in April 2021.

Fiat's rebooting problem was reported in Stephen Edelstein's article for *the Drive,* "An Over-the-Air Update Is Causing FCA Connect Infotainment Systems to Endlessly Reboot" (February 13, 2018).

Larry Vellequette quotes Audi's John Newman in his article "Audi Testing EV Post-Sale Upgrades to Supplement Future Revenues," in *Automotive News* (August 26, 2021).

William Boston quoted Accenture's Axel Schmidt and HERE Technologies' Giovanni Lanfranchi in "Your Next Car May Anticipate Your Needs," *The Wall Street Journal* (July 7, 2021).

Will GM's subscription service revenue equal Netflix's or Peloton's? Hannah Lutz has the story in the *Automotive News* article "To Drive Its Growth, GM Sees More Than Cars" (October 11, 2021), which includes GM CFO Paul Jacobson's comments. Lutz goes on to quote Scott Miller in a separate *Automotive News* article from September 29, 2021, "GM to Revamp Customer Experience with Ultifi Platform in 2023." Some of GM exec Alan Wexler's comments were reported by *TechCrunch* in "GM Aims to Build Netflix-Sized Subscription Business by 2030" (October 6, 2021).

Carfax's estimate of sixty-three million vehicles with safety operations is described in more detail in this *New York Daily News* article: "New Data Suggests There Are More Than Sixty-Three Million Unfixed Recalled Cars on U.S. Roads Today" (February 13, 2017). The National Highway Traffic Safety Administration's estimate of thirty-one million vehicles recalled in the U.S. appeared in 2010. Mike Held at AlixPartners estimated that the average cost of an automotive recall over the last ten years was about $500 per vehicle — see "Hyundai's Recall of Eighty-Two Thousand Electric Cars Is One of the Most Expensive in History," *CNN* (February 25, 2021).

Susan Beardslee of ABI Research made her comments in a post on the ABI website on March 15, 2016.

Trucks that break down every 10,000 miles were cited in this article in *FleetOwner*: "Survey: Roadside Breakdowns Occur Every 10,000 Miles" (March 18, 2019).

Tactile Mobility was profiled in this article in *Israel21c*: "Israeli Startup Helps Self-Driving Cars 'Feel' the Road" (October 17, 2018).

Pete Bigelow covered the Argo-Rapid Flow pilot in the *Automotive News* article "For Self-Driving Vehicles, a Little Cooperation May Go a Long Way" (February 20, 2021).

Amit Karp and Adam Fisher wrote about Ben Volkow and Otonomo in Bessemer Venture Partners' *Frontier* web publication in a piece titled, "Connected Cars: A Multibillion-Dollar Opportunity" (November 2, 2016).

The chapter's final quote comes from the McKinsey report "Unlocking the Full Life-Cycle Value from Connected-Car Data" (February 11, 2021).

This chapter includes my personal interviews with Cliff Banks, Reilly Brennan, Bill Cariss, Dennis Clark, Mike Granoff, Jay Vijayan and Ben Volkow.

CHAPTER EIGHT

The EVAdoption website has a comprehensive article by Loren McDonald, "What's the Future of Oil Changing Shops When Cars Go Electric?" on all things oil change (July 8, 2020).

How much profit do franchise dealers generate from their service and parts departments? NADA has that number in its "Average Dealership Profile" for 2019.

Reilly Brennan's *TechCrunch* article on maintenance and service for EVs is called "Electric Vehicles Are Changing the Future of Auto Maintenance" (March 6, 2020).

Edward Hymes spoke to *Forbes* contributor Dale Buss in "Jiffy Lube Plugs Into Electrification by Testing an EV-Service Package" (August 30, 2021).

McKinsey's data on aftermarket sales comes from the company's September 23, 2021, report, "A Turning Point for US Auto Dealers: The Unstoppable Electric Car."

Learn more about BMW's insistence on special screws in "BMW: Incorrect Glass or Electromagnetic Screws Can Affect Vehicles," *Repairer Driven News* (February 19, 2021).

Aaron Schulenberg is quoted in Brian Cooley's article in *CNET's Roadshow* web publication, "Here's Why Windshield Repair Downright Sucks with Modern Technology" (December 26, 2021).

Jay Leno quipped about EVs "not blowing up" to Emily DeCiccio for her September 16, 2021, *CNBC* article, "Jay Leno Says, 'The Electric Car Is Here to Stay.'"

Read more about LG Chem's woes in this *Reuters* article by Heekyong Yang, "S. Korea's LG Chem Shares Dive on GM Electric Car Recall" (August 23, 2021).

Jade Terreberry expects to see more recalls in Steve Finlay's analysis in *WardsAuto*, "Dealers Can Reach Extra Bases on the Recall Field" (February 22, 2021).

Audi's charge spot demonstration was described in the *Fleet Forward* article "Audi Opens First Urban Quick-Charging Hub" (December 27, 2021).

David Stringer wrote a guest op-ed in the July 2021 issue of the Automotive Ventures newsletter.

Scott Case's comments on EVs being able to command a premium was cited in Sebastian Blanco's article in *Car and Driver*, "Battery Health Reports Coming for That Used Electric Car You're Considering" (January 17, 2021).

Scott Clark's and Alexis Garcin's comments on tire impact in EVs were cited in the *Forbes* article by Jim Henry, "The Switch to Electric Vehicles Means Changing Tires, Too: Michelin" (April 12, 2021). The point that Chinese EVs could save 90 gigawatt-hours per year comes from *Green Car Reports*: "Tires Could Be Costing EV Owners an Extra Charge a Year" (October 26, 2020).

Modern Tire Dealer magazine's survey of tire industry executives appeared on May 17, 2021, under the title "What Dealers Need to Know About EV Tires."

FixMyCar's Prashant Salla made his comment to *Michigan Business Network* in the article "The Future of Auto Repair Is in Your Driveway" (June 24, 2021).

Want to know more about car washes? Check out Phil Ashland's article "Wash Trends in Auto Dealerships" on Carwash.com (January 7, 2019). Jack Allison has a good article on the same site, "Auto Dealerships and the Car Wash Industry" (December 31, 2015). Also read Bud Abraham's piece titled "What Dealers Need to Know About Automatic Car Washes" in *Auto Dealer Today* (August 30, 2006).

Autobody News has a summary of the CCC's *Crash Course 2021* report (March 17, 2021).

Lance Eliot lays out his arguments on repair work in a *Forbes* column titled "Rack 'Em Up, Driverless Cars Surprisingly Will Be a Boon for Auto Repair Market" (April 29, 2019).

This chapter includes my personal interviews with Reilly Brennan, Bill Cariss, Dennis Clark, Chase Fraser, Ed French, Andrew Gordon, Glenn Mercer, Tony Rimas and Andrew Walser.

CHAPTER NINE

The drop in net profit share of sales due to COVID-19 appears in the *NADA Data 2020 Midyear Report.*

Gallup's and Statista's infographic showing "America's Most and Least Trusted Professions" was posted by Niall McCarthy in *Forbes* (January 11, 2019).

On trust and dealerships, Babak Mohammadi spoke to *Automotive News* in 2015. Brian Hafer's AutoMD survey was conducted in 2014.

DrivingSales' Kevin Root published "How Trust Impacts Car Sales" on March 25, 2016.

TrueCar's study on what is a "fair" profit margin was posted on the company's website on June 23, 2014.

Amazon's online offerings were compiled in the joint *Automotive Ventures/AIM Group Marketplaces Report* article "Digital Retailing in Automotive Sales" (October 2020). Also see John Pearley Huffman's November 21, 2020, piece in *Car and Driver,* "Prime Mover: Amazon Is an Automotive Powerhouse."

Auto Remarketing's Joe Overby reported on Hertz's tie-in with Carvana to sell used vehicles in "Hertz to Sell Vehicles Directly to Consumers via Carvana" (October 27, 2021).

Read more about Constellation's automotive buying spree in "Constellation Claims 'Unmatched Scale' across Europe after CarNext Acquisition" by Tom Sharpe in Automotive Management's *AM-online* (October 15, 2021).

Jim Henry reported on dealers' F&I revenues in *Forbes*: "How Much Dealers Earn on Finance and Insurance: Try $1,600" (July 31, 2016).

There are more details about Lobel Financial in the report *CFPB Takes Action Against Auto Lender for Unfair Loss Damage Waiver Practices* on the website of the Consumer Financial Protection Bureau (September 20, 2021). The CFPB's takedown of California Auto Finance happened a year earlier (see the CFPB press release issued on May 21, 2021).

This chapter includes my personal interviews with Bill Cariss, Dennis Clark, Chase Fraser, Ed French, Andrew Gordon, Mike Granoff, Tim Kelly, Glenn Mercer, Tony Rimas and Andrew Walser.